Emotional In

(A Collection of 7 Books in 1)

*Emotional Intelligence, Social Anxiety, Dating
for Introverts, Public Speaking, Confidence, How
to Talk to Anyone, and Social Skills*

Emotional Intelligence

PUBLISHED BY: James W. Williams

© **Copyright 2019 - All rights reserved.**

Table of Contents

Your Free Gift

As a way of saying thanks for your purchase, I wanted to offer you a free bonus E-book called ***Bulletproof Confidence,*** exclusive to the readers of this book.

To get instant access, just go to:

https://theartofmastery.com/confidence/

Inside the book, you will discover:

- What are shyness & social anxiety, and the psychology behind them
- Simple yet powerful strategies for overcoming social anxiety
- Breakdown of the traits of what makes a confident person
- Traits you must DESTROY if you want to become confident
- Easy techniques you can implement TODAY to keep the conversation flowing
- Confidence checklist to ensure you're on the right path of self-development

Emotional Intelligence

Why it is Crucial for Success in Life and Business

7 Simple Ways to Raise Your EQ, Make Friends with Your Emotions, and Improve Your Relationships

Introduction

Emotional intelligence is extremely important and is critical for success both in personal and professional life. It helps you develop leadership skills, maintain meaningful relationships, and navigate skillfully through difficult periods of life. So, how much effort you put into developing or improving your emotional intelligence depends partly on how much you care about the quality of your relationships, and partly on how far you want to get professionally.

Emotional intelligence has become one of the most sought-after skills in the workplace, mainly because employers are increasingly looking for people who are good team-players, who work well under pressure, and who can communicate effectively in a culturally diverse environment.

Emotional intelligence can help you develop and perfect these skills by sensitizing you both to your own emotions and to those of others, and by encouraging you to constantly work on improving your relationships.

While some people are natural empaths, for most of us it's a learned skill. Those who are used to analyzing their emotions are probably also good at understanding the emotions and motives of others. In which case, they'll find it easy to develop emotional intelligence.

Unfortunately, most people are too self-centered and concerned only with their own problems and life and are simply not interested in others. Most would rather give a donation than become actively involved in helping someone, even if only to spend some time listening to them. Although this is partly due to the busy and stressful lives most of us live, it's also because our culture has only recently recognized the importance of emotional intelligence for one's wellbeing and the reasons many people struggle to develop it.

So, emotional intelligence revolves around empathy, and the ability to understand and manage your emotions. Managing emotions is about understanding the trigger that had caused a particular emotion, and not responding to the trigger until you've had time to fully understand what you are feeling and why. And when you can manage your emotions, you can manage any situation you find yourself in.

This gives you the edge over others because you are not only able to resolve a conflict before it gets out of hand, but because you know how to recognize and avoid situations which may lead to a conflict.

If, as part of your job or lifestyle, you often have to deal with a great number of people, you are probably well aware of how important interpersonal relationships are, and how good communication, or lack of it, can facilitate or complicate things.

We all have relationship problems from time to time, and what is particularly annoying is realizing, with hindsight, that many of them could have been avoided had the communication been better. This is one of the reasons why emotional intelligence is such an important skill in the workplace.

People who are in touch with their feelings can easily tune in to those of others, which helps them understand where others are coming from and why they are doing or saying certain things. In some professions, it's impossible to do your job well unless you have this skill.

Another reason why people with high emotional intelligence are such valuable team members is that they are good listeners, a trait most people lack. When you listen to someone attentively, you can hear even things that the person cannot or will not say. When you are attuned to someone, you can easily pick up subtle signs of fear, irritation, or anxiety from their body language, facial expression, or the tone of voice, all of which can sometimes be a valuable clue to what the person may be going through.

So, to be sought-after, both as a professional and a friend, you should try and develop skills which will help you cope in the high-tech, high-speed, and high-stress world we live in.

As Amit Ray said in one of his books, "As more and more artificial intelligence is entering into the world, more and more emotional intelligence must enter into leadership."

Chapter 1
What is Emotional Intelligence

Emotional intelligence is about self-awareness, self-management, and relationship management. It's about knowing yourself and being able to manage your emotions, as well as your response to those emotions.

However, although emotional intelligence can be learned, it is not something you learn in a weekend course and be "covered" for the rest of your life. This is a lifelong learning skill, that needs to be practiced and improved on throughout life.

To consider yourself emotionally intelligent, you should try to develop empathy which will make it easy to connect with others and understand how they feel. Empathetic people are those who are genuinely interested in others and who readily offer help and support to those who need it. Not everyone can put themselves in other people shoes and try to understand their motives, which is why empathy is such a valuable skill.

For this very reason, developing emotional intelligence will come easily to someone who is a natural empath or a people person. Others can learn about it in a course or from a book, but as with most other skills, to be good at it, you have to practice and apply emotional intelligence to as many situations as possible.

However, having high empathy is not easy. You have to be willing to tune in to other person's feelings and attitude, to try and understand their behavior, to listen without judgment, etc. Not everyone can do this, which is why many believe that empathy is not a skill, but a natural gift.

In other words, emotionally intelligent people are not empathic only when it suits them, but all the time. This is probably why there are very few highly empathic people around, although it's no secret that empathy can be faked, either to influence someone or for self-promotion.

Although these skills are essential for the workplace, they can also help you improve your relationships outside of work. To develop, and perfect, your emotional intelligence you have to start paying more attention to emotions, yours' and others', begin to listen more and talk less, and try to become more open to other people's point of view.

<u>4 tips on how to develop emotional intelligence:</u>

Get to know yourself

Try to understand why you feel a certain way, and what had triggered such emotions. When you know the triggers, you can either avoid certain situations or, if they are unavoidable, find a way of dealing with them. Understanding triggers help deepen your self-awareness because this helps you learn how certain situations, emotions or people make you feel, and why. It's very important you learn never to ignore your emotions, even negative ones, but to try and identify them and deal with them.

Try to understand others

Unfortunately, most of us are usually too busy to care. Life has become very complicated and competitive, as a result of which, just keeping your head above water is a challenge, let alone sharing what little spare time or energy you have with others.

Besides, in the Western culture, as well as in societies where there is a high turnover of staff and people constantly move around, regularly changing jobs and cities they live in, most of the relationships are superficial and based on interest. To understand somebody else's motives and emotions, you have to be willing to devote your undivided attention and mind to that person. You have to really want to understand their behavior and attitude, to listen attentively for hours if you have to, to be happy for them, or be sad with them.

This can be particularly hard if you are dealing with someone who is full of long-held anger or frustration. So, although empathy can be developed with perseverance and good listening skills, those who are naturally caring and compassionate are the most empathetic.

Think before you speak

Once you identify your emotion and know what had triggered it, take some time to understand it and "process" it, before responding to it. In other words, let it sink in before you react. If overwhelmed with emotions, it may help to ask yourself why you feel the way you do. When you know why something had made you feel angry, embarrassed or betrayed, it becomes much easier deciding what your next step should be.

Learn about the importance of self-management

If you learn how to identify, control, and express your emotions, you will know how to use them in a way that's most effective under the circumstances. Many people underestimate the importance of expressing their emotions in a mature way. Just like ignoring or repressing emotions is bad for your health, so is overreacting, ie expressing emotions without any consideration for how they may affect others.

Therefore, keep on reminding yourself that although held-back emotions create tension, both internally and externally, those expressed in a rush and without thinking are like shooting without aiming. The best way to improve your self-management is to have more emotional self-control and constantly work on enhancing your integrity.

Chapter 2
The Benefits of Emotional Intelligence

Emotional intelligence is believed to be one of the fastest growing job skills, and for a reason. Those with high emotional intelligence have an advantage over others in the workplace mainly because they cope better under pressure, find it easier to work in multicultural environments, and being good listeners, make emphatic colleagues and potentially great leaders.

Therefore, developing emotional intelligence makes it easier to cope with the demands of a stressful and fast-paced life of the 21st century. This is particularly important for those who see themselves in high-paid, prestigious, or leadership positions.

Therefore, the main benefit of having high emotional intelligence is that knowing how to effectively manage emotions, and being able to easily understand and cooperate with others, you stand to be an asset to whomever you work for.

Besides, emotionally intelligent people process their emotions before responding to them. In other words, they think before they speak. This may not seem very important but chances are if you have a habit of making ill-informed comments, you will sooner or later come to regret them.

This is perhaps particularly relevant for the Western culture where people usually don't like silence and tend to answer questions or make comments without thinking. Or even worse, believe that every silence has to be filled with a witty comment or a remark.

Words can both help and hurt, and your choice of words says a lot about you. So, one of the ways of raising your emotional intelligence is to become more conscious of the implications of what you are saying.

What makes people talk without thinking?

On the one hand, information overload has made us overstimulated and we find it more and more difficult to stop the inner chatter. On the other, prolonged silence easily opens the door to feelings we may be trying to keep buried, eg emptiness, hurt, frustration, etc.

However, if on the other end of the scale you have an emotionally intelligent person who can manage their emotions and use words appropriately, it's no wonder they are so often headhunted by the most reputable companies.

10 main benefits of having high emotional intelligence:

People enjoy working with/for you

Emotionally intelligent people don't harass their staff or bully their colleagues. They know how to get others to do what they want without resolving to arrogance or aggression. Being flexible and open to suggestion, they make great colleagues or leaders.

People easily open up to you

Being empathic, emotionally intelligent people can tune in to others' emotions, so they easily understand others' point of view or the circumstances which may have led them to do certain things.

You are a master of your emotions in any situation

The ability to identify, understand, and manage your emotions means you'll always be a step ahead over others when it comes to responding to challenging situations. Besides, being in charge of your emotions helps you manage stress better.

You easily resolve conflicts

The trick to successfully resolving conflicts is to deal with them before the situation gets out of hand. Your ability to manage your emotions, and easily understand those of others, as well as triggers that may have led to them, makes it possible to respond to someone's behavior in a way that will diffuse a potentially difficult situation.

Because your interpersonal skills are good, you feel relaxed around people and are not easily thrown off balance in unpredictable and difficult situations, or with unfriendly or openly hostile individuals.

You easily become a leader

Emotionally intelligent people have most of the traits of highly effective leaders: they are empathic, confident, communicative, positive, and supportive.

You can work anywhere, with anyone

Great people skills, empathy, and social awareness mean that you will be able to work well and get most out of every situation even under challenging circumstances or in a foreign culture.

You easily get a high-paid job

Being one of the most sought-after skills in the workplace, high emotional intelligence can help you get the job of your dreams.

You don't do or say things you later regret

Knowing that you have to understand and process your emotions before releasing them, means that you will only act once you've had a chance to consider the situation. Sometimes, all it takes is having a few minutes to think things over and give yourself a chance to calm down and assess the situation, before making the final decision.

If there are occasions that you are too embarrassed to think about because of what you said, or did, it's probably because at the time you didn't have or didn't use your emotional intelligence, as a result of which you made decisions you lived to regret.

You are a valued friend and confidant

Emotional intelligence skills are just as valuable outside work, as some of your most important decisions and emotions take place outside the workplace, eg with your family, in your romantic relationships, with your friends, children, etc.

You are fulfilled

Having a successful career and being accomplished personally means you will have lived your life to the fullest.

So, through affecting your emotions, behavior, and interpersonal relations, emotional intelligence has a major effect on the quality of your life.

To continually cultivate and enhance these skills, you should never stop working on your:

Self-awareness

Be constantly in touch with your feelings and learn to tune in to them.

Social skills

Cultivate your communication skills and never underestimate the power of words. Besides, to become highly empathic, you have to try and develop humility. Although being humble is not easy in a society which encourages competition and individuality, ability to openly admit your limitations and mistakes, are traits of a true leader.

Emotional regulation

Learn to control your strong emotions, particularly negative ones, and never act on impulse. Practice this by thinking of something that will make you feel hurt, angry, or exploited. Sit with the feeling, feel the humiliation, or anger, "digest" it, and only after you have calmed down "respond" to the person or situation that made you feel that way.

Chapter 3
Raising Your Emotional Intelligence

Emotional intelligence is something you need to work on throughout life. There are professions, or lifestyles, where high emotional intelligence may not be that necessary, however, most of us could do with better people skills, both in and outside work.

There are many ways of developing or enhancing your emotional intelligence. However, whichever method you decide to use, your efforts should focus on the seven simple routines which will help raise your EQ and indirectly make it easier to reach your goals, whatever they may be.

<u>7 ways to raise your emotional intelligence:</u>

Develop self-awareness

Self-awareness is about self-knowledge, about being mindful of what is happening in your life, and about having a plan how you see your career or life developing. To be self-aware you need a certain level of maturity and at least a vague idea of what you'd like to do with your life. When you know what you want, it becomes easier to find a way of getting it. If you don't, you are left drifting aimlessly, with neither a goal nor a plan.

So, how do you develop self-awareness? Start by increasing your sensitivity to your own emotions and gut feelings, as they are usually the most trusted friends you'll ever have.

Try to set aside some time for self-reflection, and reflect on your behavior, thoughts, feelings, frustrations, goals, etc.

Those who are used to self-analysis will probably find this easy, but if you are not used to this kind of thinking, this may be hard, even unsettling. In that case, start by setting aside 30 minutes every evening, once you're done with the work for the day and can relax a bit, and reflect on the day or week behind you. If you had a particularly difficult day/week, ask yourself what you can learn from the experience.

The purpose of this exercise is to get you used to thinking about how you feel and why.

Or, you may start journaling, and this is not about keeping a diary and covering your day-to-day activities and thoughts. Journaling is about writing down any unusual or frustrating experiences, thoughts or emotions you may have had. Some things are not easy to discuss with others, and anyway, not everything is for sharing, so why not get it off your chest by writing about it. The best thing about journaling is that to write something down, you have to think about what to write, and it is often this process of thinking about a problem that helps you see what is at the root of it. So, if feeling upset, disappointed or angry, write it out and move on.

Understand your emotions and what triggers them

To understand your emotions you have to be willing to feel them. It's sad how many people are afraid of their own feelings, especially negative ones, eg sadness, anger, bitterness, etc and the moment they feel these emotions taking over, they do something that will interrupt their train of thought, eg they may busy themselves with something in order to distract themselves from these unpleasant emotions.

If you recognize yourself in this, you should know that all you will achieve this way is postpone (perhaps indefinitely) facing your own demons and dealing with whatever it is that's troubling you. Emotions need to be experienced and dealt with, not buried.

Emotionally intelligent people are not afraid of their emotions. Whatever it is they feel, they stay with it for as long as it takes for the emotion to be identified. There is a reason you feel the way you do, and instead of ignoring them, you should try to "decipher" your emotions because they are trying to tell you something.

To become good at understanding others, you first have to be able to understand yourself. So, even the emotions you don't really want to feel should be addressed, processed, and let go.

Listen without judging

Good listeners are rare, mainly because this requires a lot of empathy, willingness to give up your time for others, and mental energy to be present while you are listening.

The main trait of a good listener is to listen with empathy, and that means without judging. This is not always easy, and may in some cases be impossible, so if you know you are biased towards someone, it's perhaps better not to talk to them if you know you have already made up your mind about how you feel about what they are going to say.

So, to become a good listener you should try to be present during the conversation, and stay focused. This may be hard, as some people talk a lot, or have a problem saying what they mean so you may be looking at a couple of hours. However, if you are not really interested in this person, or you are in a hurry, or are not feeling well, try to postpone the conversation for another time. The tell-tale signs of boredom or disinterest, eg glancing at your watch, or checking your cell phone or emails, can be very discouraging and insulting for the person you are having a conversation with.

Emotionally intelligent people show interest in others by encouraging them to speak more (even if they don't agree with what they are saying), and by creating an environment where it's safe to open up and say what you really mean.

So, next time you speak to someone who needs your opinion, advice or simply a shoulder to cry on, try to be patient (some people take a long time to come to the point), focused (set aside this time only for them and switch off your phone), and non-judgemental (give them the benefit of a doubt). By not judging and being open-minded, you may not only help the person by giving them a chance to get something off their chest, but you may also gain insight into what's going on in your team, or a family.

Also, pay attention to body language, both yours' and theirs', eg the tone of voice, facial expression, body posture, etc. To a casual observer, these would be clear signs how both of you feel about the conversation.

Active listening requires a lot of practice, but it is one of those skills that you can practice every day, regardless of where you are, and what it is you are listening to.

Mind-Body Connection

This is about listening to your body and understanding what it's trying to tell you. According to the mind-body connection doctrine, discomfort in a part of your body is a sure sign something is not right. For example, lower back pain is usually linked to financial problems, upper back pain to being overwhelmed with life, a knot in the stomach with fear or nervousness, etc.

Learning to notice these signals and interpret them, can save you a lot of time and trouble when it comes to understanding why you feel a certain way.

But, what often happens is that while your body is telling you that you are nervous, anxious, angry, or hurt, you simply ignore these signs, hoping they would eventually go away.

Unfortunately, Western culture pays too much importance to feeling happy and high all the time, so people are not encouraged to deal with their negative emotions, but are advised to ignore them, eg by repeating positive affirmations, or fix them, by taking something that will make them feel better. Do you really believe that if you ignore your negative feelings, repeat a mantra or take something to make you feel high, you will eventually become happy, confident, and fearless???

Sometimes, when you're overwhelmed with emotions, it

may be OK to calm yourself down, even in unhealthy ways, until you can think clearly. But, this only offers temporary relief and is not a solution to your problem.

Emotional intelligence can help you get to the bottom of your emotions by showing you how to work out what the triggers are, and how to interpret and release these emotions in the least harmful way.

Engage

How involved are you with your community? Do you volunteer? Is there someone you are regularly helping with by moral support, financially or otherwise? Are you there for others if they need you even if you know it will ruin your weekend which you had planned to spend with your family?

Empathy is the main trait of emotionally intelligent people, and it can easily be developed by anyone if they follow a few simple tips on how to develop or improve these skills. But, the best way to develop empathy is through practicing it. In other words, whenever you engage with others, you are doing what emotionally intelligent people do: you listen, you try to understand, you tune in.

However, many people fake empathy simply because they'd like to be seen as emotionally intelligent. They say the right thing, are always politically correct, appear to be full of deep empathy, listen carefully, offer help, etc. However, if caught off-guard or if for some reason not feeling in the mood for putting up an act, their true nature quickly comes out. Today, to advance professionally, especially if you see yourself as a leader, you have to prove that you have high emotional intelligence, so those who fake it usually do that for self-promotion.

The easiest way to increase your empathy is to start taking interest in others, eg how they live, what's troubling them, how they cope, etc. Improve your listening skills and try to have at least one deep conversation a month. By engaging with others, you automatically raise your emotional intelligence.

Develop self-management

Self-management is about controlling your emotions, not in the sense that you suppress them or ignore them, but learn to deal with them, and only release them after you have understood and processed them. Self-management is also about being true to yourself. Some of the ways you can improve your self-management are through developing your integrity, eg:

- Practice what you preach

- Be prepared to speak up, even if you risk being made fun of

- Don't make promises you are unlikely to keep

- Always be polite and respectful with colleagues, regardless of how close you may be

- Be self-disciplined, especially if you expect that of others

Learn to deal with criticism

Negative feedback is often undeserved and a result of the person giving it is not fully aware of your performance, or perhaps using the opportunity to sabotage your self-confidence, or openly undermine your career.

However, if truth be told, in every negative feedback there is usually a grain of truth. Although there may have been very good reasons why you underperformed or had a score of people complain about you, the fact is you failed. However, when you come to a stage when you can accept negative feedback, or open criticism, without taking it personally you demonstrate that you have both self-confidence and emotional intelligence.

So, how to become more open to negative feedback? First of all, not all criticism is equally important, nor should you react to it in the same way. A colleague's remark about your new hairstyle could be a sign she's making fun of you, but it could also be a subtle suggestion that the style doesn't suit you.

Besides, if you repeatedly receive less than satisfactory feedback on your performance, or behavior, instead of sulking or throwing a tantrum, try to look at yourself through other people's eye. What if you really ARE lazy, or short-tempered, or unreliable?

The key thing is to ask yourself why you feel bad about the feedback. Is it because it's really undeserved and a result of the person giving it not having a full picture, or are you angry with yourself for not having masked your underperformance better? Or simply jealous others did better?

Admitting you were wrong is not easy, but living in denial is even worse. So, rather than feel upset about the feedback, try to learn something from it. Especially if it's not the first time the same thing had been brought to your attention.

But, regardless of how you feel, bear in mind that negative feedback, if given without malice, can do more for your personal development, than can false praise.

Besides, there is something noble about admitting you were wrong. It may not be a pleasant thing to do, but it shows you are mature enough to take both the credit for your successes and blame for your mistakes. This may encourage others to do the same.

Closure

The world is changing faster than anyone could have imagined and what has changed dramatically in the last fifty years, is the workplace. There are many social, political and economic reasons for this, but the bottom line is the modern world requires skills that were not only unnecessary a few decades ago, but may not even have existed. So, as the world evolves, so the workforce has to keep up – the introduction of new technologies, new ways of working, emphasis on cultural sensitivity, etc.

The reason emotional intelligence has become one of the most sought after skills in the workplace, is that it revolves around the qualities essential to being successful in the modern world: empathy and ability to work in the culturally diverse environment, ability to work under pressure, willingness to embrace change, strong interpersonal skills, etc.

However, emotional intelligence is even more important for your personal relationships. When you improve your communication skills and empathy, you become more confident, more understanding, and more tolerant. As a result, you are popular because people find they can trust you and don't mind opening up to you.

When you are an active and empathic listener, you easily understand your partner's needs and feelings. And, knowing how to resolve conflicts peacefully, you avoid open confrontation which dampens many relationships. As open communication is what keeps a relationship going, you either avoid many relationship problems or skillfully resolve them in a way that doesn't put your relationship, or friendship, in jeopardy.

Besides, as you are more patient with others and more understanding of their emotions, you become better at dealing with your children or aging parents.

So, indirectly, emotional intelligence makes you more popular with friends and colleagues, more lovable to your partner, and more livable, in case you have to share a room or an apartment with someone.

With all this in mind, investing in developing emotional intelligence clearly pays in the long run. Emotionally intelligent people not only cope better with the challenges of the 21st century workplace, but being cooperative, flexible, and adaptable, they stand to succeed in all spheres of life.

So, if you enjoyed this book and believe you could benefit from a more in-depth information on how to develop emotional intelligence and cultivate the so-called critical skills that the workforce of the 21st century is expected to have, I'd like to invite you to try our book **Emotional Intelligence:** ***The 21-Day Mental Makeover to Master Your Emotions, Improve Your Social Skills, and Achieve Better, Happier Relationship.*** The book offers an in-depth, actionable tips and strategies to growing your EQ, developing the essential life skills and teaches you how to communicate effectively and positively.

You can get the book on Amazon here – mybook.to/ei21day

As Travis Bradberry pointed out, "People who fail to use their emotional intelligence skills are more likely to turn to other, less effective means of managing their mood, and are twice as likely to experience anxiety, depression, substance abuse, and even thoughts of suicide".

Social Anxiety

Easy Daily Strategies for Overcoming Social Anxiety and Shyness, Build Successful Relationships and Increase Happiness

Introduction

Congratulations on purchasing *Social Anxiety* and thank you for doing so.

The following chapters will discuss what social anxiety and shyness are and give you strategies to manage your social anxiety and shyness.

Despite being very similar, the conditions are different from one another. In the first section of this book, we will look at the psychology of how they are different and where they come from. The similarities between the two conditions will be examined, and the process the brain goes through when the feelings of shyness and social anxiety flare up.

The second section will offer tips, tools, and strategies to prevent social anxiety- related panic and manage shyness in a social situation. These strategies may be different from what you've read before, but they are all simple and easy to adjust in your daily life.

You have probably read other books and visited websites to find help for your shyness and maybe you have asked professionals for insight. You have probably reached the point that feeling awkward and tense around others means you begin to avoid social situations. Have you ever had your mind go blank in the face of talking to new people? Do you have a hard time making lasting, meaningful relationships? This book will help you find out *why* you feel this way and *how* to manage the feelings.

Emotional Intelligence

There are plenty of books on this subject on the market. Thanks again for choosing this one! Every effort was made to ensure it is full of as much useful information as possible. Please enjoy!

Chapter 1: Social Anxiety and Shyness Explained

Social anxiety and shyness are both psychological misfires in the brain, but social anxiety goes deeper than shyness. Social anxiety is the fear of being judged in a negative way by others, while shyness is a feeling of being awkward or tense around others. Both have a root cause of fear - fear of being judged, a fear of saying the wrong things, but they each come from very different parts of the mind.

Social Anxiety Disorder means that the person experiencing it has such fear of social situations that they either suffer through them with a high level of strain on their emotions or avoid social situations entirely. They experience deep fear of being humiliated or judged for anything they may say or do, or even what they wear. While some people who suffer from social anxiety are shy, it is not the case with everyone. Statistics show that only approximately 50% of people who have social anxiety claim to be shy. Oftentimes, people with social anxiety want to participate and be able to talk and have lasting, meaningful relationships, but their fear of humiliation and thoughts of anxiety inhibit their ability. They also feel very negatively toward their anxious feelings, continually mentally berating themselves when they experience their symptoms. Living with social anxiety can also mean other mental disorders as well, such as depression, drugs or alcohol addiction, and eating disorders.

Shyness is actually considered a character trait. Most people who are shy do not consider it a bad thing about themselves.

These people do experience anxiety and worry about saying or doing the wrong things, but while it does inhibit their behavior somewhat, they are able to maintain a steady mood without the loop of irrational and negative thoughts. Shy people tend to get past their social concerns once they become more familiar with their surroundings. While being shy is not the same as social anxiety, shyness can evolve into social anxiety under the right conditions. Allowing your shyness to keep you from joining in on new things, letting your focus fall on thinking negative, and withdrawing from your circle of friends nurtures the conditions under which you will begin suffering from social anxiety. Additionally, having unrealistic expectations or drawing irrational conclusions about an upcoming event could exacerbate your shyness and transform it into social anxiety. Going into a situation expecting to be rejected or focusing too intensely on your anxious reaction will only serve to make it a self-fulfilling prophecy, and a feeling of failure afterward.

Biologically speaking, social anxiety was necessary for prehistoric days when living outside of a tribe meant essentially, death. In the civilizations where everyone contributed their skills and were a part of a tribe's culture for hunting, gathering, and homesteading, being "strange" or "too quiet" meant that a person was often avoided or even cast out of a tribe. Being conscious of one's thoughts, actions, and words were important in keeping one's tribe. Tribes also had to be able to communicate with one another in order to grow and not die out, so they had to be aware of what would make members of other tribes shun them. Therefore, it makes sense that social anxiety has prehistoric roots, because of those roots and the amount of time it takes to evolve traits in humans, social anxiety, and shyness are an inherent part of our genetics.

The feelings we get of anxiety or shyness in new or stressful situations is set off by what's called the "fight or flight" response - the intuitive reaction your mind automatically engages when you are faced with scary situations. The "fight" response makes you want to stand your ground and face down what is in front of you. The "flight" response makes you want to remove yourself from the situation immediately so as to avoid the inevitable danger that set off the response. For most people, this response is programmed properly and does not activate during innocuous situations such as a new study group or, say, a blind date. However, in some cases, the fight or flight is set off in the face of these same situations.

These are not feelings that you can just force down. It's something that you have to work on to retrain your brain to recognize the anxious signals and head off the automatic fear response. Your mind's reflex is to react adversely when you are confronted with a situation that makes you uncomfortable socially. In order to be able to overcome what is holding you back, you have to first become aware of what is triggering the reaction, then work to mitigate the negativity associated with it.

When someone makes statements like, "Don't overthink it" or "Don't be silly, you're fine!", or even, "It's all in your head. You don't have anything to worry about," you can pretty well know that they have not experienced shyness or social anxiety. They don't understand how hard it is for you to simply show up to a gathering and keep an expression besides abject fear or unyielding stress on your face. They don't comprehend how courageous you are just to be out there, facing the fear that makes your mind reflexively try to fight or flee.

There are also cases of a chemical imbalance in the brain. The chemical in the brain called, *serotonin,* manages the regulation of moods and emotional reaction. In cases of social anxiety, the production of serotonin in the brain has been found to be either dampened or grossly underproduced. This causes the irrational feelings of nervousness and fear, as well as making it difficult to come out of those feelings without conscious effort. While an underproduction of a brain chemical is a physiological matter, you can use psychological efforts to boost this level with some practice. While there are medications available to treat social anxiety, they are only meant to be temporary solutions, and sometimes there is not a good fit between you and the medication (meaning, it doesn't work), or the side effects are worse than the ailment the medication is treating. Some people simply do not want to take prescription medication. A physiological reaction may be the cause of your anxiety or shyness, but that does not mean that the only solution is pharmaceutical drugs. In the next section, we will discuss natural and sustainable ways to overcome and manage your social anxiety or shyness.

Don't let this get you down, though. Even though social anxiety and shyness are part of our genes, that doesn't necessarily mean that we're doomed to stay stuck with these conditions that don't serve such a dire purpose in modern times. Our genetics determine how our bodies and minds react in situations based on past experiences and what our adult guardians taught us growing up.

Fortunately, your mind is adaptable and once you get down to the bottom of what causes your anxiety and shyness, you can work through those things and overcome the problem.

In order to get to the root of your fear, you first have to become aware of it and how it begins. Does the thought of meeting new people make you sweat? Do you become quiet or say awkward things in a group? Is it difficult for you to hold a conversation?

What happens in your mind when you are facing a situation that normally makes you feel shy? What is the first thought that springs up? If you are worried that you won't be able to hold a conversation, think about why that is. Your past experiences are what shape your current thoughts, so there is something possibly in your unconscious mind that makes you think you can't hold a conversation. Even if you can't immediately come up with the *why*, you can become aware of your thoughts when your anxiety starts and work back from there.

You may experience physical side effects of anxiety and shyness. Aside from the sweaty palms and racing thoughts, you likely have a hard time not only thinking of things to say but actually going through to form the words and engage your voice. You get tongue-tied. Then, your cycle of negative thoughts and feelings become compounded by this negative experience, leading to more anxiety and a harder time overcoming the anxiety in the next social situation you face.

Thoughts are not initially negative or positive, just like social anxiety doesn't come out of anywhere. However, it is the emotion brought on by the thought that is designated negative or positive, and that emotion is a conditioned response from previous experiences, either from your own personal experience, or the experience of a trusted person in your life. When your mind recognizes the negative emotion attached to the thought of social situations, it begins the cycle of negative thoughts. When thoughts occur in the brain, they have to find a neuron to travel down to appear in your working mind. If that neuron has a negative connotation to it, you are more likely to experience anxiety, fear, or sadness associated with that thought.

Here is where shyness and social anxiety differ. A shy person may experience a slightly elevated heart rate, and some worry about if their hair is in place. Whereas a person with social anxiety experiences sweating, a notable increase in heart rate, a feeling of not being good enough, and a solid fear that everything they say or do will garner a negative reaction. Feelings of shyness generally lessen after a time of being in a social situation; however, a person with social anxiety will not get relief from their fears until the social stimulation is gone.

A shy person probably comes from a family of at least one or two people that are shy and nervous. Someone suffering social anxiety is running off the memory of frequently overexaggerated-rejection and extreme social awkwardness.

Social anxiety is learned, while shyness is a part of someone's personality.

Shyness and social anxiety have some repercussions that may affect a person's life. If you have social anxiety, you probably avoid most social situations if possible because you know it will cause you a high amount of stress. If you do attend, you stay off to the side and don't talk to anyone because you feel like no one would want to talk to you or they would think you are strange. A shy person could miss out on an opportunity to network for their job or meet that special someone because their nerves didn't dissipate quickly enough to act. A person with social anxiety might have those same missed opportunities but would put themselves through a mental lashing for not being able to go after them due to their anxiety.

Depression can also be caused by social anxiety and shyness. Since a part of social anxiety is avoidance of social situations, it instigates isolation. When you are isolated, you are staying away from the friends and family who can help you come out of the cycle of negativity and sadness. You are limiting your opportunities not only to make more memories and friends but also practice the many ways to overcome your fears. Your quality of life is affected in ways that seem small but could actually have larger consequences than you realize.

Think about it - if you are shy, you are less likely to approach people. If you can't talk to people, meeting a new friend or special someone is difficult. Approaching your boss for a raise or promotion is not as probable to happen if you are shy. You will not branch out your social network, which means you miss out on adventures and stories that your other friends have (along with a richer quality of life.) You could miss out on the opportunity to become a valuable employee and earn more money. If you are shy in school, you have more of a probability of poor school performance simply because you can't manage your anxiety. Poor performance in school has a lasting lifetime effect on your life.

Shyness and social anxiety inhibit your best self. If you have tried other advice and still find that you have more shyness or social anxiety than you'd like, you will want to read the next section to see how to identify what begins your shyness and anxiety, as well as ways to manage them or beat those feelings altogether.

Chapter 2: Shyness and Social Anxiety Managed

There are many ways in which overcoming and managing your social anxiety and shyness can be mapped. Most experts agree that Cognitive Behavioral Therapy is a good place to start, but there are other, smaller things that you can do in your daily life to make adjustments that will relieve your feelings.

As stated in the previous section, in order to master your anxiety, you first have to find where it comes from. What was it in your past that started to make you feel as though you were not good enough, smart enough, and cool enough to be in public around people? Did you have a presentation at school that didn't go as you'd like? Was it that time you asked out your middle school sweetheart and she said no? There is some triggering event for your social anxiety that needs to be uncovered so that you can examine it and work through it.

That being said, shyness may not have that same type of initiation. Maybe you've always been the quiet kid or the kid who blushes when girls talk to you. Where people with social anxiety have a starting point, people who are shy tend to be born that way or encouraged to be quiet as a young child. Knowing the difference between the two conditions as well as being able to differentiate which you suffer from, is key to learning best how to cope since they have different starting points.

Although, the conditions sometimes do overlap, as in the case of symptoms and physical expression. Both have symptoms of sweating, not being able to think clearly, higher heart rate, blushing, and trembling. If you can't use the prevention tools that will be discussed, there will also be a section for management or stopping the symptoms when they happen. Both conditions also have a knee-jerk reaction of retreat or avoid, which will be discussed also.

However, while they are similar in some respects, they are different in others. Sometimes treatment for shyness is different than the treatment for social anxiety, which can be more involved than shyness. We will discuss strategies that will work for both social anxiety and shyness, then more specific strategies for social anxiety and shyness.

A good place to start getting over either shyness or anxiety is being mindful. Staying aware of where you are, what is going on around you, and keeping your focus on the person talking to you will help distract your mind from its anxious thoughts. If the forefront of your mind is staying in the present and actively listening to what your conversation partner is saying, it is easier to keep the conversation going. The bonus here is the person you are talking to will feel like you really are interested in what they have to say. Imagine how handy that will be when you are talking to potential romantic partners! By keeping your mind and focus on them and not zoning out, trying to come up with your responses, and looking them in the eye, you are communicating to them that they are important to you. Moreover, what love interest doesn't want to feel important and cherished by their significant other? The intrinsic (inner self) bonus is that you will be able to talk and concentrate without letting the fears and concerns rob you of the here and now when you are most wanting to be present. Your anxiety and shyness are, essentially, drowned out. You will be able to enjoy your friends and be there for their actions so that you can be a part of the story and not someone who had to hear it second hand. Imagine how great it would be, the potential memories you will make when you are fully present and not worried about what's happening in your head. Being mindful is a great step toward overcoming the shyness and anxiety that is holding you back while being just a small daily adjustment you make in your mind.

Self-help manuals can also help if there are a clear and easy-to-follow premise and relevant exercises for you to do. Obviously, the manuals you have read up to this point have not done what you needed of them, so maybe it's time to try some external, physical, and visible work. Get a manual from a reputable psychiatrist or group. Usually, books from university psychology professors are very helpful, because many of the strategies and thought processes they write about are things they see every day, if not employ themselves. They are reading (and assigning!) case study after case study, analyzing them, interpreting them, and are able to see the scientific data that backs up what their book is claiming. If you flip through a book and can't tell what the author is trying to help you do, it is probably not a reputable (or effective) book, so move on. Sometimes self-help manuals are used in conjunction with therapy, but for the purpose of this book, a good self-help manual is something you can take 10 to 15 minutes each day to read from and put the advice into action. Keep in mind, though, that self-help books only work if you follow their directions, whether or not you feel the author is credible. If you choose this route, be prepared for using self-motivation to stick with it. Of course, you have already come across something that motivated you to read this book, so that shouldn't be too much of a problem with the right book.

Talking seems like it might be counterproductive as a legitimate way to address shyness and social anxiety since it means talking to a person, (technically, a social situation), but it is usually more cathartic to share your burdens with someone else. You don't have to tell them every detail of your day or experience unless you just want to. The purpose of talking isn't to raise your anxiety or shyness, but instead, help manage the feeling that spring up when you are in situations that make you uncomfortable. Talk with someone who knows you, and who you can trust not to make you feel bad about your experiences. This way, you will have someone there you know you can trust, while you practice getting a handle on the physical symptoms you experience when your shyness or anxiety flares up. This is very helpful simply because when you talk to someone who understands how you feel, you don't feel so isolated in your thoughts and feelings. You are not keeping toxic feelings and information inside your body but putting it out into the open so that you don't feel like you are carrying the weight of the world and maybe getting some legitimately helpful advice. Talking is a simple, effective action that can help you overcome your anxieties.

Practice confidence in yourself and pay attention to how it makes you feel on the inside. Sure, you might have to fake it at first out in public, but, hey, you're out in public. You didn't let your anxiety keep you locked away in your house. That in itself should be a good confidence boost since you have already proved to yourself that you are capable of setting aside your concerns. Once you have something positive to build on, authentic confidence becomes easier to achieve. When you walk, don't stare at the ground. When you talk, use a clear voice. Make eye contact with people to show them that you are important. If you help yourself feel important, that feeling will grow with the more you are able to do it. Positive behavior can be just as easy as negative behavior once you practice enough.

Journaling, or simply writing down your day, can be extremely effective in helping you become more aware of your feelings before, during, and after social situations. That will help you learn what your triggers are so that you can either become more comfortable in the situations where they come up or work around them so that you don't have to face them and allow the anxiety to spark. It doesn't have to be drawn out, or something that you do each and every time you have a feeling of anxiety or shyness, but just 10-15 minutes a day spent reflecting on what happened during that day will be almost as effective as talking to someone without the fear of them judging you if you really, truly feel that you have no one you can talk to.

Treatment for social anxiety apart from shyness is different than trying to overcome both conditions. Sometimes you are socially anxious in situations where you would enjoy being an active participant rather than a passive bystander - that is not you being shy, that is the negative thoughts and feelings that cause your anxiety taking up the forefront of your mind. In light of this, some more in-depth treatment may be necessary.

When learning how to manage social anxiety, one good way to get started on conquering it is through trying things out of your comfort zone. Consider where you are comfortable: are you ok poolside with two close friends? Can you handle a party as long as you know the host? Once you figure out your limit, consider what the next step would be. Could you hang out at the pool with someone whom you don't know, as well as the two friends you normally hang out with? Try it. Stay present and be focused on what's happening around you. Try going to a birthday celebration at a restaurant for a co-worker. Try little new things to expand your comfort zone and help you face your fears. Conversely, never stepping outside your zone can make it shrink, which will only make the social anxiety worse - the opposite of your goal. Sure, you will be uncomfortable, but that's the point. You are working toward expanding the scope you are currently living in. If you never try something uncomfortable, can you really say that you've done all you can to get over your condition?

Social anxiety is often triggered by an initial thought, which then attaches to a memory and subsequent emotion. Part of treating social anxiety is tracking down that thought and that memory. The memory that supports a thought as negative is most often hidden behind the anxiety, which understandably makes it difficult to see and work through it. Stick it out and find out what sparks your anxiety. Were you bullied as a kid and now you fear being picked on again? Did you enter the science fair with an amazing project including demonstration and didn't win? After tracking down and working through the negative memory, you may even find that the memory you had was flawed and blown out of proportion. Understanding where your negative thought comes from will enable you to remind yourself that the memory is flawed, and you can let the feeling of anxiety go without having a physical reaction to it. Doing this requires you to be aware of what is on your mind when your anxious thoughts begin. When you recognize the signs of impending social anxiety, you can avoid the anxiety from spinning out of control because you are able to reign in your mind before it gets out of control.

Take stock of what matters. You are a valuable, brave person with a lot to offer. In the grand scheme of things, people are mostly wrapped up in their own problems and don't have time to worry about if your shirt is tucked or untucked. Ask yourself if the judgment of others is practical when the apocalypse starts. After all, you're the one with the safe bunker and everyone else just wants a corner of it.

Confront your negative feelings. Ask yourself, "Is this response realistic or do I need a reality check?" "Does it hurt anyone if I show up like this?" or "Is there a parachute nearby so that I can bail if I need it?" Is it possible that you are only projecting that there will be a disaster? By questioning your feelings, you are making yourself think from another, more grounded perspective, which allows you to come back to the present reality.

If you feel that you don't have social anxiety, but you are shy and want to change that about yourself, there are some small things you can do as well.

The old saying "fake it 'til you make it" is still offered as advice today for a reason. Training your mind to lean into a more positive mindset is made easier when you are already portraying yourself as confident. You already know what it looks like to be confident, and even though you might fake your confidence at first, your brain will become attuned to how you are acting and can move easily into that feeling in a more genuine way. Your mind starts to acclimate itself to the outward appearance and if you can go into a situation believing it will go well, you will be looking for the openings to make the situation feel better for you instead of focusing on how awkward you feel.

Watch the self- criticism. As a shy person, you tend to be harder on yourself for not participating more or being as "normal" like your best friend than you would be if you were not shy. This also leads to lower self-esteem and a higher risk of depression. Be mindful of the way you talk to yourself. Would you talk to your mother that way? If not, then it's not nice enough to say to yourself. Don't make the mistake of undervaluing yourself or everyone will think it's okay to capitalize on your lack of self-worth. If it's not sweet to say it about your mother, then it's not acceptable to be negative about yourself.

Don't call attention to your shyness, either. First, it sets you up with any new people around you to try and take advantage of you being shy. Broadcasting that you are shy is equivalent to wearing "I'm insecure" on a sandwich board in the middle of Times Square. Calling yourself out gives the expectation that you will say something awkward and the people around you would have an excuse for avoiding you. Second, pointing out that you are shy can lead people to expect that you will say or do something that doesn't present well with your actual self. Many times, shyness is overwhelming in your mind but not visible on the outside, or, at least, so mild that the new person in your group may never even notice.

These are just a couple of ways to manage or control your social anxiety. Start with these tips and move to more detailed ones if you find that you are still too shy or too anxious in social settings than you would like to be. There are many resources available to help with both social anxiety and shyness, including workbooks and effective exercises that work on getting you out into the world.

Conclusion

Thank for making it through to the end of *Social Anxiety*. Let's hope it was informative and able to provide you with all of the tools you need to achieve your goals of being free from shyness and social anxiety.

The next step is to get out there and practice. Use the starting points in Chapter 2 to help you beat your anxiety or shyness. You know the *why* of social anxiety and shyness and the *how* of getting past the feelings. Now it's time to put them to use. Social anxiety and shyness do not mean you can't lead a full, rich life. You can beat the challenges presented by social anxiety and shyness.

DATING SECRETS FOR INTROVERTS

Discover How to Eliminate Dating Fear, Anxiety and Shyness by Instantly Raising Your Charm and Confidence with These Simple Techniques.

INTRODUCTION

If you have accepted the social tag "introvert", congratulations! You fall into the elusive category of one of the most sought-after men in today's dating game. Of course, you may not be feeling very sought-after right this minute. At the end of this introduction, you might realize that you may have missed out on more opportunities with the ladies than you know because you weren't paying attention. First, let us answer the impertinent question of why introverts are ranking higher on most women's "hot list".

Introverts have this general air of mystery to them and mystery in a man is woman magnet. Add this to that highly sensitive nature that characterizes most introverts (think Ryan Gosling in the movie, Drive), you create an irresistible aura. There is also statistics supporting the theory that introverts are less likely to cheat than their more outgoing peers. Put all of these together in one person aka you and it is not hard to understand why you have become the ideal mate.

So, if you really are that much of a big deal, how come numbers (or ladies) are not falling on your lap? Because you are meant to lead in a relationship. This is not bigotry, it is just the way of things. If you tend to get asked out a lot by the ladies, you will discover a disturbing pattern in your relationships. It is either you find yourself settling for less than you deserve, or you are at the whims of someone controlling.

It is possible to be true to who you are and still take an active lead role in your relationship. Sometimes, all you need is the green light. Not every woman has that direct I-want-you-to-ask-me-out gaze but here are a few things that might indicate the lady (or ladies) are interested.

1. You make eye contact from across the room a lot and there is a spark every time you lock gaze.

2. She genuinely enjoys talking to you

3. Her arms are relaxed or wide open when she is talking to you

4. She hints at plans for the future that involve you

5. She is following you online and actively likes or comments on your posts

CHAPTER ONE
DRESS THE PART

The main tool required for opening conversations with women is confidence. A guy may have no exceptional body features and even look like he got dressed in the dark but with plenty of confidence, he can charm the most stunning woman in the room and walk out leaving said woman (among others) hanging on his every word as if her life depends on it. Not everyone is born with that level of confidence. However, everyone can grow their confidence level to enable them to initiate that one conversation that could change their lives forever.

The basic confidence builder is appearance. Granted, we cannot all look like Tom Cruise physically or have enough money to fund a cosmetic transformation (I wouldn't recommend it anyway). So, beyond visiting the gym to whip yourself into shape, there isn't much you can do about your physical appearance. You can, however, play up your appearance with clothes. With a little guidance and careful investment in your closet, you can infuse your style sense with your personality and show the world who you are.

There is a general saying that applies to life and to dating as well. Stylists and fashion gurus are quick to dispense the phrase "dress to impress" to eager fashionistas and while it may be applicable in certain context, in the dating game, it can prove to be fatal. This is because it is only possible to impress someone you know or in the very least have an idea of what their likes and preferences are. In your case, you have not even met or started dating yet, so how can you truly impress her?

My advice is dress for you. Wear what makes you feel confident. Get well fitting clothes. Choose colors that work well with your skin tone (yes, there is such a thing). Wear patterns that don't make you look overwhelmed and avoid clothes that make you nervous and fidgety (because you are not comfortable). It is unattractive and throws your confidence off balance. The best fashion advice I ever got was from my father. Always dress like the best version of you. In other words, dress to impress you.

A lot of introverts like to dress for comfort and while this is applaudable, this "comfort" dressing tends to morph into a casual homeless look that does not really communicate who you are underneath all those layers (or lack of) of fabric. Again, I am not asking you to dress like you just stepped out of a page of a GQ magazine (although that has its perks). All I am saying is that you pay attention to your clothes. Before you throw up your hands in despair, I took the liberty of including some fashion pointers to help you get started on your new fashion journey. They are simple but if applied, could make a significant impact in your style.

1. Press your shirts

It is amazing the difference putting iron on your clothes could make versus when you wear them with wrinkles and all. It doesn't matter if the shirt spots a designer label or not. Wrinkles on your clothes makes you appear careless, cheap and certainly not date worthy. Ironed clothes on the other hand gives you a sharp and distinguished look even if it is just jeans and t-shirt.

2. Pair patterns and colors cautiously

Using certain colors together have a clownish effect and while everyone may like the clown, not many women are eager to go home with one. Don't get me wrong. Women love guys that make them laugh. But nothing can shrink your confidence faster that finding out that she is laughing at you rather than with you. As a general rule, try not to wear more than 3 predominant colors in one outfit.

3. Know what clothes are appropriate

Showing up at a black-tie event in jeans and biker boots might excite the rebel in you but it is also a one-way track to becoming isolated at events that is if you ever get invited at all. Sure, you want to express your personal style in your outfit but, it is important that you know what belongs where. Besides, with accessories, you can add that personal touch that stands you out without making you the odd ball.

Unless your fashion journey involves professional stylists, it may take a while to wear you in the fashion sense. You may have some trial and error experiences along the way but with each attempt, you gain more confidence. Beyond boosting your confidence, dressing well creates a good impression of you which is essential when you meet new people. It may sound unfair, but your dressing helps formulate people's opinion of you. So, don't be afraid to begin this process. It is time to show the world the sophisticated and more confident you.

CHAPTER TWO
GET OUT OF THE HOUSE

For an introvert, dating might involve you doing the exact opposite of what you love to do which is meeting people. This might be a daunting experience for even the bravest of men but, you have to start from somewhere. As you make a foray into the social scene, it is important you pay attention to your scenes carefully. Brazenly walking into a hot night spot might be akin to ripping the bandages off but the "sensory" overload can have some serious backlash resulting in the decision to "never again". My recommendation? Baby steps.

Start by visiting places that interests you. If you are an art lover for instance, places like the museum and gallery could provide a more positive experience. That is because, it holds things or events that appeal to you. Also, in these kinds of settings, you might run into people who share similar interests. People with similar interests mean you have more to talk about and when you have more to talk about, you give yourself and your prospective date a chance to really get to know each other. If nothing else, at least, you get to indulge in something that you actually like.

Choose places you are familiar with. For the proper introvert, there is no familiar place like home. And with Netflix and chill as legitimate dating options, we don't necessarily see the need to go out. It would be kind of me to point out here that the Netflix and chill date only happens when you have an actual date. Unless dates have started falling out of the sky and straight into your living room, you will have to go out. But, it doesn't have to be too far from home. Your favorite coffee shop could be a good spot. You are familiar with the waiters; the menu and this kind of familiarity might make you less self-conscious. The less awkward things are, the better your chances of scoring her number (and possibly a date if you put your best foot forward).

Go out in packs. Ever been to a bar or a party and seen that weird guy in the corner casting weary glances across the room and giving out awkward body language in his poor attempt to strike a conversation? Chances are you have been that guy. It can be hard to pitch a lady when you have that sad cloud hanging over you. Having a social pack can help you feel as part of the group without having to do anything beyond being there. This gives you a chance to scope the room for prospective dates and zero in on your interest. Plus, if your buddies are the outgoing type, they could get that initial awkward conversation out of the way and help you enjoy your time out.

I am going to skip ahead here and take you to a possible scenario where you have been set up on a blind date. There are a lot of mixed feelings when it comes to blind dates. For starters, it could be a relief to have someone else set you up. All you must do is dress up, show up and hope to God it works. On the other hand, it can feel awkward. Like how you are at lunch with your best bud and then this other girl shows up and then your friend suddenly has to "attend to an emergency". Painfully awkward. I would vote for the former.

If you are lucky enough to have friends who set you up with the ladies, please accept. It may not lead to "the relationship" right away but, it gives you the chance to practice.

HOW TO SURVIVE A BLIND DATE

1. Try and get a little information about your date. People who meet through online dating platforms have more leverage in this regard as you spend the pre-date period chatting to get to know each other.

2. Choose somewhere where you will both be at ease.

3. Plan to keep things short and sweet. Not all dates turn out to be great. Plan on something that would not prolong the agony if you end up in date hell.

4. Don't shy away from unconventional dates. Be open to trying something different. Just be sure to give your date the heads-up too.

An interesting date option for me during my early dating years was choosing an activity instead of a place. Traditional dating requires people sitting at a table over a meal and talking to get to know each other. Typically, I am quite comfortable doing the listening while the lady does the talking but after a while, most ladies assume you either don't have an interesting life or you are just not interested in sharing. So, I decided to show my personality instead of just telling her about it. Sailing was something me and my buddies did every other weekend. And so, for a date, I invited Sara on a boating trip.

I had 3 of my closest friends and their girlfriends over. It was a crowdy scene but, Sarah got to see me in my element in the company of the people I am most comfortable with in the whole world. It was my comfort zone and featured activities (apart from eating) that I was interested in. Barring the ear-piercing scream Sara let out when she caught a fish, I would say that was my most successful first date ever. By combining all the elements of a great first date; comfort, familiarity and great company, I was able to get over the awkward first huddle and actually enjoy getting to know someone.

CHAPTER THREE
STEP OUT OF YOUR COMFORT ZONE

After all the grief I gave you in the previous chapter about staying with the familiar and sticking with what you are comfortable with, I can understand your confusion here but, stay with me. I am taking you somewhere. In the beginning, I talked about taking baby steps. You don't wake up one day a baby who can barely flip over on their stomach and then the next day you are running down a flight of stairs. It starts with carefully learning to coordinate your muscles, gain mastery over them, having a few practice tryouts and before you finally take a plunge.

In this case, first, you work on boosting your confidence by paying attention to your appearance. Then, you start going out to familiar places. After that, you explore a bit more. To improve your dating prospects, you need to widen your search pool. Social dating apps are great as they connect you with people you probably would never have met otherwise but, it also has the great disadvantage of keeping you confined to your comfort zone. You need to go out there and really experience life even if that may sometimes mean sharing that experience with other people. Being an introvert, I understand how you would prefer our own company to anyone else' but if you are going to date, you are going to start liking the company of other people too.

Now that we have established this, here are a few additional benefits of stepping out of your comfort zones

1. You get to know yourself better.

Trying out new things puts you in a position to test your limits. How can you tell you are not going to like Indian cuisine if you have never really tried it? Life is happening outside the walls of your room and going out there is one of the best ways to live it. The flip side of the coin is that by stepping out of your area of comfort, you get to discover if your introversive nature is linked to social anxiety or if it is even more deep rooted than that. Whatever the case, each new experience reveals a new layer of you.

2. It enriches your life.

There is no question about it. Not all is good and right in the world and there is a 50% chance that your quest to find a date could be a horrific experience ranging anywhere from mild drama at the table to psycho date from hell. But, in the kaleidoscope of life, the good and the bad adds more "flavor" to your experiences and makes you better for it. Imagine the stories you would share with the grand kids (if you are into that sort of thing).

3. It improves your confidence.

Trying out something new for the first time whether is an activity, visiting a new place or meeting new people, is a daunting task. But, it is an excellent confidence builder. It is kind of ironic when you think about it. That in facing your fears, you overcome them and with each victory, you become bolder and more confident. The psychology behind it is that in facing your fears, your find your strengths. Look it this way, to build muscle mass with workouts, you need to push your muscles past that comfort zone. In the same way, to bulk up your confidence muscle, you have to try something new.

4. You might actually enjoy it!

This is a no brainer. The moment you get past the mental barriers such as fear and anxiety, you might be surprised by how much you enjoy it. Hanging out with the boys after work may (in the most positive way) prove to be a more fulfilling experience than the crew from that Comedy Central show who keep you company every week night on the couch. And if not, there is always that record button. It always comes in handy.

So, we know that stepping out of your comfort zone has these fantastic benefits but what does it really have to do with dating? We started this journey with a purpose. To whip out your charm and raise your confidence to the optimum date maestro levels. Remember that ship and harbor quote? A ship at harbor is safe but that is not what ships are meant for. You are not meant to sit back on your couch night after night hoping that you miraculously run into your soul mate on your way to the washroom. Try out at least one new activity every day and in the spirit of taking baby steps, I made a list of simple tasks you can start with. Be sure to add to the list and keep at it daily.

- Try a new coffee flavor at your favorite cafe

- Maintain a 2 second eye contact at a perfect stranger and smile at them

- Compliment the first girl you see in the morning (your dog or cat does not count)

- In your outfit of the day, include one brightly colored item

- Push your curfew time by one hour

CHAPTER FOUR
TAKE THE INITIATIVE

This is the part where a lot of introverts lose their nerves. They work up the courage, boost their confidence levels only to become tongue tied at the point of communication or completely abandon ship altogether. But that is not going to happen with you because you have me. And that is saying a lot! Let us demystify this cloud that hangs over the task of asking out a beautiful woman. We will start by getting the worst out of the way. You dread her response. But here is the only thing that can happen, she would either say yes or no.

I have never heard of someone who got smacked in the head for trying to scoop a pretty woman. Well, unless you were rude and obnoxious, or a husband or boyfriend happened to be close by and in that case, you should politely tell him you were just paying her a compliment, then back off and move on to a woman who is available. But, let's not debate scenarios because that is how you lose your courage in the first place. Instead, let us look at the two most likely responses you would get. Anything else would fall in the less than 10% category.

Nothing deflates one's ego faster than the word "No". Well, I can think of a few things but, let us keep things sanitary here. You have done the work, put in some really good effort into your appearance, visited the familiar and unfamiliar and now that you are feeling confident, you walk up to your dream girl and she just turns you down. It doesn't matter if she said a few nice things to soften the blow (well, it helps), it still hurts anyway. But here is the real deal, this is the worst that could happen.

If everyone threw in the towel every time they heard the word "no", many of us wouldn't have been born. You should not give up. There is a twisted version this advice I just gave you were guys are encouraged to keep pressurizing the said girl until she caves in and says yes. That is just creepy and wrong in every sense of the word. When I say you shouldn't give up, I meant don't stop trying to find your dream girl. She is out there. Because, one of the most defining qualities of your dream girl is that she thinks you are her dream guy. You deserve nothing less. So, if you enter into the dating game with this mindset, you would understand that no simply means, she doesn't see her mate in you ergo, she is not the one.

Admittedly, it is a downer, but you shouldn't stay down. Be okay with it and don't take it as a personal affront. However, if you pay attention and play your cards right, there are certain things you can do to improve your chances of getting a yes.

1. Before you make your move, you can actually tell if she is into you or not. I talked about this in the introduction. Subtle nuances and body language can indicate interest. Of course, this is not 100% foolproof but, it helps.

2. Don't try to be cocky or over confident. It is okay to fake it in certain situations but not this one. Ladies can smell a phony for miles. Be yourself and you would find that those

clumsy gestures and stuttering might be a redeeming quality. I know you would rather do it without the awkwardness but if this is who you are own it.

3. Choose your words carefully. A lot of times, those pickup lines your read about in dating books could leave you falling flat on your face. There are conversation starters you could use to break the ice. They don't have to be lewd or suggestive just genuine.

4. Do a quick check or have your buddies do it for you before you make your movie. Look sharp and make sure that there are no lingering evidences of your salad in your mouth. And most importantly, check that there you are not wearing the all-natural "eww de cologne". It is difficult for a lady to say yes to bad breath and body odor.

In the next likely event where this magical lady says yes to you, all I can say is congratulations! You have found a special woman. But, your work is far from done. In the next chapter, we explore ideas for your first date, navigating first date hurdles and provide practical tips on how to keep the conversation flowing.

CHAPTER FIVE
KEEP THE CONVERSATION GOING

Right after asking a girl out, the next panic inducing problem is what to do on your first date. You want everything to play out perfectly like a montage from those romantic chic flicks. Unless you are in an actual movie or you have the event planner for the British royalty on speed dial, you can kiss the perfect date goodbye. That is not to say you should expect Murphy's law to take effect either. I am just saying that you shouldn't sweat the small stuff so much that you break out in a rash. Sure, you want to make sure that she has a great time. That is noble, and your heart is in the right place. But, you should also make sure you are having a great time too. If both of you are enjoying yourselves, the date qualifies as a success and you can go on to making other plans.

Traditionally, most people like sit downs at restaurants. Or picnics in interesting places. These days, people have come up with more unconventional ideas. From hiking popular trails to visiting famous landmarks. Unless this is someone who runs in the same social circle as you, you may need help in sorting this one out. In the time that you have secured your date, I am almost certain that you secured her number too. The straight forward approach would be to ring or chat her up and ask her plainly if she has any ideas for where she might want to go. If you are lucky, she may have a specific place in mind. The problem with this kind of approach is that you have a 50% chance of her suggesting somewhere above budget or a place with bad memories for you. You can either agree to it or recommend somewhere similar based on her preference.

The romantics would prefer a different approach. You want to figure out your lady and sweep her off her feet with grand gestures. That is all great, just be sure that you don't get swept out the door for your efforts. The key is to be genuine and remain true to yourself in all that you do. You are still getting to know this person. Figuring them out is part of a process that takes more time that a first date would permit. Let the unraveling of each other be in the experiences that bonds you guys together.

No matter what route you chose, the one thing that matters is that you show up and show up on time. It is rude and unacceptable to keep your date waiting. If she starts acting out even before the starters arrive, I can't say I blame her. I have fumed at clients who treated me with less respect. You could offer to pick her up to avoid this. And if you find that you are running late even by 1 minute, pick up your phone and call her. This way, she knows that she is important to you and she doesn't feel disrespected.

With the whole feminist movement, it is hard to tell if your chivalrous gestures might be interpreted as insulting or caring. I would say, be who you are. If you naturally chivalrous, by all means be chivalrous. Whatever the case, be at your best behavior. Stand when she stands and sit after she is seated. Pull out her chair if that is your thing (I personally think every guy should make it their thing). And most importantly be attentive.

The next part is starting a conversation and keeping it going. The general rule of keeping conversations is asking open ended questions. These are questions that require more than a yes or no response. But in asking your questions, try not to let things segue into an interrogation at a job interview. Keep the questions light, interesting and please try not to be a critic. That is like third date move. The subject of religion, political affiliations and sordid pasts should be left for subsequent dates. You can talk about interests, passions and anything else that bring the spark to both your eyes. Be a good conversationalist. Give as good as you are getting.

Keeping date conversation going is a very delicate balance between body language and use of words. This may sound like plenty work. But if you relax and try to have a good time, the rest would come to you naturally.

CLOSING

Love is a beautiful thing and when you find the right person for you, it is worth every social hurdle you had to overcome to be with this person. From experience, I can tell you that those things you are afraid of are more often than not in your head than a reality. You have created these mental barriers that keep you from living the life you are meant to live. You deserve to be happy, but you must make up your mind to create your own happiness even if it means doing the things that scare you the most. The pluses far outweigh the cost and your life would be richer for it.

Use each day to learn new things about you. Open yourself a little more. Smile more. And don't assume that everyone out there is judging you for who they are. And even if they are judging, you know that their opinions don't count so why would want to live your life for them anyway. Commit to living each day in the most authentic version of yourself. Because, it is when we are truly who we are that we find strength, confidence and love. Remember, you deserve the best.

Public Speaking

10 Simple Methods to Build Confidence, Overcome Shyness, Increase Persuasion and Become Great at Public Speaking

Introduction

If you have ever listened to a great speaker then you can attest to the fact that there's something that's not only inspiring but also uplifting when sitting before a poised and polished public speaker. Public speaking may come naturally for some but it's also an art that can be learned and mastered. Mastering public speaking is beneficial in diverse ways as it precipitates self discovery, builds confidence and also triggers self expression.

Effective communication skill is considered as the backbone of the society and can be used to influence decisions, form connections and motivate change. Effective speaking enhances one's ability to progress in their personal and work life. Great public speaking is a skill that every business person should consider developing in this competitive environment. It takes great speaking and persuasion skills to gain customers attention for increased sales and business growth.

As much as public speaking may come naturally to some, the fear of public speaking is one of the common phobias that many people contend with on a daily basis. It's a kind of performance anxiety that can be quite paralyzing but the good news is that whether public speaking comes to you naturally or you feel a rise in anxiety whenever you're faced with an opportunity to speak publicly; the principles shared in this book has the potential of transforming you into a world class speaker.

There are loads of information on public speaking that have been shared. However, finding a resource that takes you through a step-by-step process from a state of fear and anxiety in public speaking to a state where you get to hear applause from the audience after delivering a speech is what this book focuses on. **Public Speaking: 10 Simple Methods to Build Confidence, Overcome Shyness, Increase Persuasion and Become Great at Public Speaking** is a book that has covered in detail what it takes to become a great public speaker.

The book has shared in-depth insight on understanding the context of public speaking, building confidence, speech creation, vocal preparation and all that you need to do in order to become a great speaker. You also get to learn the 10 simple methods that you can use to build confidence and influence effectively and become a master at public speaking. Whether you are already a pro at public speaking or you are just getting started; there are valuable nuggets in this book that can help you with your journey to becoming great at public speaking.

Chapter 1
Understanding the Context of Public Speaking

Ideas are considered as the currency of the 21st century and public speaking is critical if one is to succeed in selling their ideas persuasively. Communications in its various forms pervades the current business environment as much as many people tend to overlook the importance of effective communication. With many people struggling with insecurity about public speaking; having knowledge of what it takes to deliver a great presentation can be liberating. Once you master the art of public speaking, you will be more confident in your abilities to deliver a more dynamic presentation and fire up your audience in a way that they find to be irresistible.

Public speaking cover a wide genre such as facilitating a meeting, stage presentations, interviews, training sessions, arguments, answering questions, negotiations, making calls, working with clients and more. Whether your focus is in enhancing your professional growth, inspire and persuade your audience to take some action or even take your business to the next level; you need ways that you can use to convey your ideas in a more clear, captivating and structured way. Regardless of your level of communication skills, you can become more confident, more impressive and more competent as a speaker.

Speaking can be viewed in two parts, creating a talk and performing a talk. Creating a talk entails everything you do before you speak while performing a talk entails everything that you do as you engage in speaking. Effective communication is therefore achievable when one manages to master both the two parts. One may be a great speech writer but lacks the confidence to say what they have written. Another person may also be comfortable with speaking but lacks valuable things to talk about. One may also think that they are great at both even as their audience strongly disagree. Regardless of your skill level, you can still improve in your public speaking skills.

 Most people can clearly remember listening to a person giving a great speech or presentation however, it becomes harder to identify and even synthesize the elements that constitute a powerful speech. There are various factors that constitutes to a great speech; it could be because the topic being discussed is of interest to the listeners. It could also be that the speaker is authentic and engaging. An authentic public speaker can be perceived as engaging in ways that surpasses the context of the subject in discussion and that can in turn give the message an element of significance that it might have lacked.

Learning how to speak and being able to present authentically with the intention of conveying to the audience the information at hand is critical. In order to bring out a more authentic self in delivering a great speech consider the following;

Understand the Context

Context refers to the actual space that you are to speak in. You should be able to understand your audience and be able to gauge beforehand their interests. Public speaking requires that you have an audience that's willing to listen and also engage with you. Carrying out an audience analysis will in turn lead to igniting greater audience interest, improved credibility towards the speaker, and a more receptive audience.

Be Yourself

We are all different and unique in our ways and to be authentic, you have to know how to be yourself whenever you're in the spotlight. Trying to imitate someone will only make you display an uncomfortable body language that might not be consistent with what you're saying. Avoid emulating the techniques used by others and instead let your experiences and personality guide you as you present. In doing so, you will be making the right steps in ensuring that your listeners are receptive and are also willing to consider thoughtfully the content of your presentation.

Understand your topic

There are different contexts of public speaking and despite the circumstances you find yourself in, it's advisable that you have good understanding of the topic that you intend to speak about. When you have understanding, you will then focus less on thinking about what to communicate and how to engage with the audience. The more time you spend with your content for better understanding the more confident you will be while speaking on the topic.

Never be afraid to improvise

Regardless of how well you plan, things may not turn out exactly as you had planned. Public speaking can at times be unpredictable right from the faulty projectors to last minute changes. A public speaker should be able to improvise whenever something turns out in an unexpected way. It could be a malfunction of the presentation equipment which makes it impossible to display visuals. It could be a question from the audience that you're unsure of how to answer. You don't have to sweat, just develop some composure and try to be flexible so as to think of ways to improvise.

Play to your strengths

People are gifted differently; there are those who are great story tellers. There are also those capable of bringing life into any raw information they speak about. Others are great at using their body language and mannerisms to ignite engagement with the audience. Just know that there is no right or wrong ways to deliver a speech. Great speakers are capable of identifying their strengths and using them as tools to create a presence that's relatable and authentic. While preparing to deliver a speech, you also need to determine ways that you can use your strengths to connect with the audience and you will come out as a more authentic speaker.

Benefits of developing effective public speaking skills

- Creates opportunities for career growth

- Positions one as an authority in a given field.

- Provides an edge above the competition

- Ability to market products and services to larger audiences effectively

- Ability to assume leadership and impact others

- Motivates and persuades others to attain professional goals and take relevant actions.

Chapter 2
Building Confidence

Confidence is one of the most important attributes that you can have as a public speaker. It is an over-arching attitude, a feeling about oneself that enables one to speak with an assured sense of authenticity. With confidence, one is able to see the best of every situation in a clear context. One is able to trust their public speaking abilities and also feel in control of the situation. A lack of confidence stem from an individual's early development. It also comes from the childhood experiences and the way in which you remember them. To build confidence, one has to be ready to change their behaviors which in turn change the signals to your brain that affirm your value and self worth.

Being fearless as a public speaker entails a mix of both passion and authenticity. To be confident as a public speaker, you need to ask yourself a few questions such as "How can I become fearless as a public speaker? How can I become confident in public speaking? When your adrenaline sets in and you become nervous, it affects one's ability to act normal. Building confidence entails being able to get through public speaking without showing the audience that you're nervous. Most public speakers struggle and stress over trying to be fearless and confident irrespective of how they feel inwardly.

They in the process fall into the trap of pushing the nerves away to express a feeling of being confident. What happens as one struggle to push away the fears is that they end up sabotaging themselves and in turn fails to connect with the audience. Powerful public speaking may start with talking from the heart even if you are not 100% confident. Instead of pushing the feelings of fear away, you can find a way of using the energy for good. Being fearless as a public speaker is not necessarily a lack of fear; it's more about taking the fear and transforming it into energy and excitement around your message.

To build confidence in public speaking, you can follow the below steps;

Positive Mental Image

Psychologists have stated that those who are deeply confident as public speakers tend to have a positive mental imagery that reinforces confidence. If your mental imagery expresses lack of confidence then that's what reflects in your speaking. To develop a positive mental image;

- Practice picturing yourself speaking. Look out for the senses that get stimulated. What do you hear, smell or see? Do you feel nervous or confident? What is it in your mental imagery that makes you feel that way?

- Play the positive mental image of you speaking and picture yourself looking from out of your body. Try to change the colors of the room where you're speaking and see what happens to your level of confidence. How do you see the audience? Are they sitting or standing? Are they close or a bit far? Adjust the audience the way you want in your mental image until you begin to feel confident and powerful.

- Are there people in the audience that are not receptive? Picture them with some clown nose and see if it makes you feel more confident. It may sound inappropriate but just do it anyway.

- Feel the reaction of the audience. Do you hear silence or laughter? Picture a firm grounding of the floor in your mental imagery, something that will make you feel more confident.

- Practice these shifts mentally whenever you think of giving a speech. The practice will enable you to rewire your neurological habits of your brain so as to access your confidence.

Visualizing public speaking success

Begin seeing yourself presenting with confidence. It's important to note that your present perception of yourself and your abilities is a belief structure. So if you believe that you lack confidence then that's what you will experience unless the belief is changed. Remember that your actions and behaviors can help with altering your beliefs. To visualize speaking with success;

- You can close your eyes and imagine yourself breath in confidence while you exhale fear. Practice breathing in and imagine yourself walking with confidence within the room.

- See yourself engaging with the audience positively. See yourself speaking and the audience looking amazed at how smart and informed you are. Go through the entire speech with the same feelings.

- As you conclude your message, revert to yourself and think of how confident and powerful at public speaking you are. Look at the audience exuding excitement and thanking you for your words.

- This is the place where your confidence lives and it's your power to public speaking.

Slay the inner critic

The inner critic is the negative inner dialogue that keeps popping with negative messages. It has a way of diminishing one's confidence in public speaking if you believe it. I could emerge from statements that you were once told such as "you sound terrible when you speak," "You have a bad accent" and such like. To overcome negative inner dialogue, you have to be aware of them. You can do the following;

- Focus on your past successes with public speaking even if you aren't experienced yet.

- Replace the negative inner dialogue with something positive and empowering.

Develop a fearless stage persona

Confident speaking is not about imitating anyone or putting up an act, however it can still help with adopting a stage persona that enables one to stretch into the fearless parts of their being. To develop a persona that's fearless, you should ask yourself the following questions;

- What are the best qualities that you have as a speaker? Are you compassionate, focused, or cool? Are you great at change or a powerful peacemaker?

- What might your trademark features look like? What do you do with your hands as you speak? Are you slow and well calculated with your movements or more energetic as you move about the stage? Identify these unique internal traits then develop them and utilize them in making your public speaking confident and second to nature.

Mix the ingredients up

Great public speakers have a mix of certainty and confidence that uniquely belongs to them. They are the actual creators of their confident speaking as the fearlessness is not given by anyone. They choose to build it by honing their skills through practice and preparation. Everyone has the ability to feel the sense of power and the deep confidence that comes with believing in your message.

Chapter 3
Speech Creation and Delivery

To become great at public speaking, one should have a clear understanding on how to create and deliver a speech. In public speaking context, creation of a speech refers to researching, organizing and outlining the information that you intend to present. Once you have created your speech, the next step is to work on delivery. Delivery is what determines whether one is a great speaker or not.

 It's through delivery that you get to communicate your confidence and your level of preparedness to the audience. Effective delivery is what shows your audience that you have researched the topic well and you understand what you are talking about. As much as delivery is something that should be happening at the moment of expressing your speech, effective delivery needs to be laid before one step into the podium.

To create your speech, you should follow the below steps;

Research and preparation

Take time and consider the audience that you are to speak to and ensure that the tone of your speech and information is appropriate for the audience. Put yourself in your audience shoes and think of what you may want the outcome of your presentation to be. Take time and gather as much information as possible on the topic you are to speak on.

Overcome Anxiety

Speakers at times do experience anxiety in many ways such as shaking hands and legs, rapid speech, voice fluctuations and sweating amongst others. To effectively deliver your speech, you have to overcome anxiety. As a public speaker, your goal should not be focused towards eliminating any form of apprehension; you can use them to invigorate your presentation. Having apprehension may act as a motivation for you to prepare effectively. It can also make you have the alertness and energy that in turn makes your presentation to be interesting.

Write your speech

Planning is critical if you are to deliver a successful speech. Ensure that you plan what the opening and closing statements should be and how you intend to transition through the different phases of speaking. Here are steps you can follow as you plan your speech;

- Begin with an attention grabbing fact. It can be a rhetorical question, a quote or any relevant anecdote. The opening speech should be something that grabs the audience attention.

- Keep a positive attitude and tone and ensure that you take a short time.

- Tell the audience what the problem could be, propose a solution and the actions that the audience can take to help.

- Plan a conclusion that summarizes the main points then finish up with a motivating and strong appeal for action. Ensure that you inspire your audience

Practice

It's through practicing that you will be able to know your speech so well so that you can speak naturally as you glance occasionally at the notes. One of the biggest mistakes that many people make is failing to rehearse their speech enough. If you intend to give a compelling speech that has the potential of inspiring the audience to listen to your call to action then you have to spend plenty of time in preparation.

Here are some tips for practicing;

- Practice your speech as many times and ensure you do it before a friend for feedback. You can read the content aloud either with a friend or to yourself then make adjustments until the structure starts to flow and sound natural and conveys the message.

- Speak clearly and add gestures, eye contact and movement for more impact. Just ensure that you remain relevant and natural with the movements. Practice the movements, props and body language until you are accustomed to the moves.

- Do a rehearsal with the actual outfit you intend to wear. You can invite a few friends and family to watch you give the presentation. Try to avoid sticking to the podium. It may act as a barrier between you and the audience. You can put the notes on it then try to walk around as you speak.

Set the tone

Tone generally refers to the feeling or the mood that the speaker creates. A speaker's level of confidence, attitude and emotional state is generally revealed through the tone of voice. The tone of voice is therefore a powerful tool that enables the speaker to engage with the audience, charm and even encourage them to listen. There are times when the tone is set by the occasion, such as speaking in a wedding or a funeral may require different tones. Wearing a smile or a happy face as you get up to deliver your speech helps with setting the tone of friendliness and warmth.

If you look tense and serious then you also set a different tone and it could be one of discomfort and anxiety. Remember that you get to set the tone for your presentation long before giving the speech. The tone that you set should be in a way related to the speech you are about to make.

Language style

As a public speaker, the language style that you use in giving your speech shapes your speaking style. The language style is the vocal part of your nonverbal communication and it refers to pace or speed at which you're speaking, the pitch of your voice and the volume. Style may also refer to the type of phrasing that a speaker uses and the effect it creates. You should speak in a clear and precise way that the audience can clearly understand what you're expressing. Avoid mumbling and use of language that complicates the sentences.

Improve your language style by steadying your breath and reflecting on your pace. You can also elevate your speaking style by incorporating metaphors, simile and hyperbole in your speech. You can also consider using parallelism, repetition and personification for a better understanding of your speech. Have a vivid imagery as you bring your point across.

Put the visual aids together

Visual aids are important aspects of your speech and can help in making unfamiliar information to be more accessible to your audience. You can use power point presentations, charts, videos and even photos to get your point across. You can keep the following in mind as you prepare visual aids;

- The visual aids that you use should be simple and also colorful. You should however remember that color green and red may be difficult to read from a distance.

- Keep the text to a minimum otherwise your audience may be confused on whether to read or listen to you. Use of a few charts or slides can help your audience understand the message however too many slides can be distracting.

- Videos provide a powerful way of passing information and you can consider that as well.

Handling Q&A

The way you handle questions and answer sessions can in a great way strengthen your credibility as you get to demonstrate your knowledge. The Q&A session also gives you the opportunity to clarify and also expand on your ideas. To handle the session effectively you can do the following;

- List down possible questions that the audience may have in reference to what you are presenting and prepare the answer as well.

- If anyone in the audience is becoming antagonistic or aggressive then you can simply say that you'd be happy to talk about the matter in greater depth afterwards as you have limited time and you need to address other questions. Never allow anyone to take control over the presentation.

Vocal Preparation

For effective public speaking, you also need to pay attention to your vocal variety. Vocal variety refers to the variation in your tone, the speaking rate and pauses as you speak. You need to vary the way you speak so that you don't sound the same all through the presentation. It's the variation in your vocals that will keep your audience interested and engaged in your presentation.

Keep in mind the vocal projection and ensure that you speak loud enough so that your audience can hear you well. Making eye-contact is another way you can use to show engagement with your audience. Use eye contact to create your persona and it can also add some credibility to your presentation.

Chapter 4
10 Simple Methods to Public Speaking Mastery

Public speaking is a crucial ability that people should consider mastering not only for the sake of giving powerful and memorable speeches, it can also improve one's chances to success in business. The ability to express thoughts in a more convincing, clear and concise way can make a huge difference in one's life regardless of what they are involved in. Here are the simple methods to public speaking mastery;

Unleash the Inner Master

A great public speaking should have a combination of both mindset (internal) and behaviors (external) factors. If you possess all the right behaviors but lack the right mental attitude then your audience will notice the incongruence and the presentation may come out as fake. Great speakers begin with a strong self belief as they define the purpose of their speech and what they intend to achieve for both themselves and the audience. Even as you work on your oratory skills and impressive body language, ensure that your mindset is right with positive self talk.

Practice the Art of Story Telling

Human minds are wired for stories and great public speakers use stories to grab the audience attention and hook them to the speech. People love listening to great stories and stories in a way have some hypnotic effect on those listening to it. People are more likely to forget important things in the speech but they may not easily forget the story you shared. The story however should be simple and also relatable. The story should also present a clear point of view if it's to be considered as effective.

Personal stories are considered to be great since they are credible and has the potential of inspiring action. Even as you tell the stories, remember that it's about the audience even if it's a personal story. Make the story to be clear and figure out how it can help the audience and why it's important. Your speech will not only be interesting but will equally empower and inspire your audience. Great speakers use storytelling in their presentation as a way of;

- Making important points in the speech memorable
- Establishing connection with the audience
- Introducing issues that may be controversial
- Shaping beliefs and raising levels of energy within the audience
- Motivating people to act

Focus on the audience and ignite a conversation

When engaging in public speaking, it's important to know that you are not talking to a crowd but a group of individuals. Each person within the room expects you to connect with them, reach out and even impact them individually. So consider igniting a conversation, make eye contact and speak deliberately in different parts within the room. Try to speak to each individual's special concerns.

Stay in the moment and be mindful of your audience, focus exclusively on their needs than on your desire to look good.

Deliver Captivating Moments

To create an emotional appeal, you should speak from the heart. Whether you are delivering a humorous talk or telling a story with the potential of moving the audience and connecting with your speech, purpose to speak from the heart. Pay attention to your body language and the vocal cues. Great public speakers are always aware of their voice and body language. Ensure that you contrast the change in your tone and body language to reflect the emotion and importance of what you're saying.

Grab attention and close with dynamic end

The first words that you get to speak when you start a conversation can either turn them off, send them to sleep or grab their attention. Start your speech with an attention grabbing statement knowing that you have just a few seconds to gain their attention. Instead of spending the first moments in thanking the hosts then flipping to your power point slides which automatically turns the audience off; consider starting with a quotation; a statistic or even ask a question. You can also tell a short story as you get started.

You can conclude your speech with a strong statement that your audience is likely to remember and a summary of your speech.

Stick to 18-Minute Rule

The science behind the 18-minute rule has been proven to be effective for public speakers and is a common practice with TED speakers. Giving people too much information can result into cognitive backlog and the more information one is required to retain the more they are likely to forget. If you have to give a presentation for more than 18 minutes then you should have mechanisms of reengaging the audience frequently. You can allow the audience to ask questions, share videos or stories as a way of reengaging them.

Engage all the 5 Senses

Great public speakers know how to connect, engage and also persuade their audience using the five senses. To be effective as a speaker engage your sight by making eye contact with as many individuals within the audience as possible. Activate hearing senses by playing music either at the beginning or end of the presentation. To engage the thought, you can ask a question that the audience can contemplate over. As for the speech, engage by telling stories that are relevant to the subject. Engage touch senses by greeting people either before the presentation or after as they join to get started. You can also engage touch sense by patting someone in the audience as you speak and remember to wear a smile.

Study the Masters

One of the best ways that you can use to become a great speaker is by following leaders, those who have mastered public speaking. There are several videos of exceptional speakers online that you can use to improve your public speaking skills. You can determine your area of interest and fully immerse yourself into learning and researching about the field so as to emerge as an expert in the field. Follow thought leaders and strive to stay in touch with the latest trends.

Let your personality shine through

Be true to yourself by showing your passion. Avoid imitating other people even if you love their style. Be authentic, conversational and energetic. When you express your passion and believe in your topic it will show to your audience. You will be able to establish greater credibility if you allow your personality to shine through. Your audience may also get to trust you if they perceive you to be real. You don't have to master all that you have learnt at once just grasp a few and keep putting them into action as you deliver your speech.

Fail Forward

To be great in public speaking you should not shy away from failing. Trying not to fail may hinder you from succeeding as a great speaker. Great public speakers are known to take chances and also make calculated risks of reaching their audience and sharing ideas. Avoiding being on the spotlight just because you failed and choosing to stay in your safe place may only hinder you from becoming that great speaker. Begin by speaking in small meetings such as kid's events, small gatherings and church

To be great at public speaking, you need to keep learning and improving your public speaking skills. You can join famous organizations such as toastmasters as they help people learn on how to deliver great speeches. Members learn by rotating in giving speeches and they also receive feedback from the group. The organization also helps with creating some sense of accountability and a safe environment for practice.

Chapter 5
Developing Persuasion Skills

Every public speaking opportunity provides one with a chance to shine and a chance to build their profile and brand. Persuasive speaking entails winning people over by combining use of words and ideas to change people's mind. Persuasion involves directing, appealing to the thinking and guiding an individual or an audience. The goal of persuasion is to enable the audience to accept the idea, action or the information being shared by the speaker.

To be able to effectively persuade, you should have a good understanding of your audience. You should get some insight on their needs, wants and their desires in relation to your ability to fill the needs. Consider their view point and figure out what you would do if you were in their position. Let go of the expected outcome and focus on their best interest and how you can help them realize it. There are three elements to being persuasive as a public speaker and mastering them can enhance your persuasion skills;

Ethos

Ethos entails the credibility or the character of the speaker. In order to be asked to give a speech, share your observations, thoughts or make a presentation publicly as a speaker, you should be expressing some level of knowledge and authority in the given area. Before you get to convincing your audience to take some action there are aspects of credibility that you should look into such as below;

- Does the audience express respect towards you?
- Does the audience believe in you being of good character?
- Does the audience see you as trustworthy?
- Does the audience view you as an authority in the area of your speech?

It's important to note that your audience should be able to see you in this light if you are to persuade them successfully.

Logos

Logos is synonymous with making logical argument and it entails the logic behind the conclusions that are drawn by a speaker. To ensure that the speech is well understood by the audience it has to be conveyed in a logical, informative and clear manner. To ascertain whether your speech is logical, you can consider the following;

- Does the speech make sense?
- Is the speech based on statistics, facts, or evidence?
- Will the call to action lead to the expected outcome as desired?

Pathos

Pathos entails the ability to create an emotional appeal or a connection between the speaker and the audience. The speech should have the potential of capturing and holding the audience attention and for that to happen the speaker should be able to create emotional connection with the audience. Emotional connection can be achieved in diverse ways such as sharing a story, anecdote, simile, analogy, metaphor and analogy. The message being shared should be linked to the emotional trigger in a way that ignites response from the audience. You should be aware of the feelings that your words evoke. Ask your words evoke love, fear, compassion, hate, contempt and such like.

Conclusion

Congratulations and thank you for reading the book all through to the end. Now that you have insight on what it takes to become great at public speaking; you should take the necessary steps of putting into practice what you have learned. Follow the steps shared and the actionable tips and ensure that you should practice.

As shared in the book, it takes practice to become a great speaker, don't be discouraged with failure. Keep getting out and putting yourself into the spotlight as it will just be a matter of time before you start reaping the fruits. Whether you are already started with learning the art of public speaking or you are just considering it; **Public Speaking: 10 Simple Methods to Build Confidence, Overcome Shyness, Increase Persuasion and Become Great at Public Speaking** is a book that has been written with you in mind.

Make use of the information shared to hone your skills and remember to keep learning as you sharpen your skills. You will be amazed by the benefits once you master the art of public speaking.

Thank you and enjoy your journey of becoming a great public speaker!

Confidence

Simple, Proven Methods to Manage Anxiety and Shyness, and Transform Your Personal and Professional Life

INTRODUCTION

What would it be like to become a confident person and a great conversationalist? How do you get past the paralyzing fear that grips you every time you want to talk to a group of people? Wouldn't it be nice to be at the center of attention for once? If you want to overcome your shyness, take charge of your social life professionally and personally, then read this book. *Confidence: Simple, Proven Methods to Manage Anxiety and Shyness, and Transform Your Personal and Professional Life* explores social anxiety in depth and provides practical tips that will transform your life.

Anxiety and shyness go hand in hand. If you suffer from acute shyness, you are not alone. There are millions of people all over the world who share the same problem. It is a general knowledge that people who suffer from acute shyness tend to live a lonely life, isolated from friends and family. And even those who manage to come out of their shells are only ever really themselves with a handful of people. This doesn't have to be the case with you. What you are holding right now has the power to change your story.

This book is not about a magical formula that can instantly transform you from shy Sean to Brazen Boris overnight. It is based on sound psychological principles that have been applied in regular scenarios by shy people. Each step is detailed and outlined in very uncomplicated terms. While the results vary in degree, the final outcome is an experience of increased confidence in the individual and a more positive outlook on life.

There are many proven ways to overcome shyness and this book addresses the most effective methods. From discovering the real reasons behind your shyness to uncovering mental barriers that keep you from living a fulfilling confident life, this book is designed to peel back the layers of myths and facts about shyness and put you in charge of your life. In this book, you will understand

- The key factors that influences your anxiety and makes you incredibly shy

- 5 reasons why being shy actually makes you a better person

- How to cope with anxiety in stressful situations

- Ways you can make yourself relevant in the workplace

- How to overcome shyness in social settings

This book is not just another self-help manual to swipe off the shelf and store at the bottom of your magazine rack. It explores scientifically proven methods of coping with social anxiety using simple and easy to follow steps that can be applied to day to day scenarios. Essentially, if you are ready to meet the super confident new you, turn over to the next stage to begin your journey.

My History with Shyness

Shyness is something I have struggled with for a better part of my life. It crippled my effectiveness in the workplace, ruined my relationships with a lot of people I cared about and left me emotionally exhausted even before my day began. I dreaded the thought of going out and interacting with people. I would wake up and within minutes, I was already wishing for the end of the day. Now, I know that this book isn't about me. But, I wanted to start off by saying that if I was able to get past all of this, so can you.

Overcoming shyness for me was a series of steps that I took over the years that gradually built me up to the point where I was very confident in myself and impressed with my social skills. I decided to catalogue that experience and compress it into this book. However, instead of spending all that time in achieving the transformation that I had, I created a point by point agenda that speeds up the process for you. However, I must emphasize here that reading this book is one thing, applying its principles is another. If you want to see a change, you must be willing to do the work.

I wrote this book with the hope that you can see the potential in yourself to be better. Not because there is something wrong with you but because you deserve to be happy. But happiness doesn't just waltz in to your life. You are responsible for creating your own happiness and this book is a roadmap that will guide you to your destination.

Understanding Shyness and Anxiety

Life is full of instabilities and uncertainties. And because of this, we worry about possible outcomes. This is normal and comes with the territory. However, when worries overpower other emotions and interferes with your daily routines, it veers into anxiety. The good thing about anxiety is that it is very easy to diagnose. There are clear symptoms of anxiety and you can make a prognosis without a doctor present. There are mild forms of anxiety and then there are also severe cases. The greater the sense of worry, the greater the anxiety levels.

Shyness on the other hand is a tendency to feel awkward and anxious in social settings especially if it is in an unfamiliar environment with new people. This awkwardness in shy people is rooted in the worry about what other people think about them. Social anxiety stems from low self-esteem and lack of confidence in one's individual abilities, personality, physical traits or even possessions. Shy people almost always have a tendency to project their own insecurities on others. This projection makes it difficult to build new relationships with people. Thankfully, anxiety is easy to treat just as it is easy to diagnose.

SOCIAL DISORDER ANXIETY OR JUST SHYNESS

As I mentioned earlier, there are both mild and extreme cases of anxiety and you might need a little help deciphering what level on the social anxiety scale your anxiety experience falls under. The following are common signs of anxiety;

- Sudden profuse sweating
- Restlessness and a strong urge to flee from the situation
- Rapid heartbeat or palpitations
- A sense of dread and impending doom
- A rush of thoughts [most of which are unwanted]

These are clear signs of anxiety but how can you tell if your shyness is amplified by your anxiety or if you are suffering from a social anxiety disorder? According to statistics, more than 15 million people in America suffer from social anxiety disorder (also known as SAD) which is a form of phobia for social settings. That number quadruples exponentially when you look at the global figures. There are no clear markers for symptoms of SAD other than the fact that all the symptoms mentioned earlier are experienced by the sufferer in varying intense degrees.

Whether you are experiencing the more common form of shyness or you are an SAD sufferer, you are not entirely helpless. By understanding the root of your problems and reversing certain patterns of behavior, you can overcome your shyness and learn to be more confident in social setting. Let us look at how anxiety and shyness affect your life.

NEGATIVE IMPACT OF SHYNESS AND ANXIETY

You may be working with the assumption that your shyness doesn't really hurt anyone but, unless you face what it costs you, it may not be possible to develop the courage to overcome it. I drew up a list of 5 major ways shyness negatively impacts your life

1. It can lead to loneliness

People who are very shy know this well. We tend to keep to our company not because we find ourselves super fascinating (which we do sometimes) but because our shyness keeps us confined to ourselves. Shyness makes it extremely difficult to form satisfying relationships with other people thus causing us to lead lonely lives.

2. Renders you unable to cope in new situations

Nothing sends a shy person running for the hills faster than the prospect of facing a new situation. Even when the current situation is unbearable, a lot of shy people would rather remain in it citing the adage, "better the devil you know than the angel you don't" as their reason.

3. Causes low self-esteem

When in a crowd or small group of people, the predominant thoughts of a shy person is usually negative. Bordering on things like how they are not good enough or dressed well enough and they see these thoughts reflected in the people they interact with even if there is no reason to feel this way. Consistently brooding on negative thoughts like these takes its toll on the individual's self-esteem.

4. Affects your confidence

Having a low opinion of yourself is a one-way ticket down to no-confidence villa. Where you second guess your thoughts, your ideas, your looks and basically everything about you, it becomes even a chore to even summon the courage to get out of bed daily. It is like have a loud cheerleading team inside of your head. Only, instead of cheering you, they are booing you.

5. People get the wrong opinion about you

It is easy for people to meet a person who seems averse to meeting new people and quickly jump into the conclusion that they are snobbish. The fact that you seem to be turning down every invite you get does not help improve that opinion of you either. There are situations that would require you to speak up but, because of your shyness, you don't. Your silence may be misconstrued as consent and your entire perspective on the subject is misunderstood.

But, shyness isn't all doom and gloom. There are positively beautiful traits that shyness breeds in a person and it is important to highlight them here.

1. Shyness make you a great listener

Your tendency to leave the talking to the other party involved can seem like laziness on your part. On the contrary, it creates a sense of trust that makes people want to confide their deepest and most intimate thoughts with you because you listen.

2. It makes you more sensitive to the emotional needs of others

Shy people are experts at observing the people in their environment. And because they are more observant, they pick up on nuances and body language that cues them of the true nature of the emotions these people are experiencing. You may consider yourself invisible in social settings, but invisibility comes with a gift. The ability to see through emotional masks.

3. You are the best kind of friend

It is not easy for you to make friends so when you eventually do, you value your friendships enough to treat them right. You are loyal, caring and sensitive to the needs of your friends and these qualities can be attributed to your shy nature. However, we should not discredit the fact that you are simply an awesome person and once people get to know you, they almost never want to let go.

4. You think before you act (or speak)

Most shy people don't react emotionally. At least not without thinking through their actions before they do. You are rarely caught in a situation where your voice decibel is high and people other than the person you are having a conversation with can hear you. And this is good. People could take lessons from you.

5. You have a calming effect on people

One of the unique personality traits of shy people is that they have learnt the art of internalizing their feelings. So even in stressful situations, they appear calm and collected (they might be a sweltering mess underneath but the keep the chaos there). People see the calmness and tend to mirror that because they are made to feel calmer. Of course, internalizing your feelings is not the best way to go but, for all intents and purposes, it works.

Emotional Intelligence

Coping with Socially Triggered Anxiety and Managing Shyness

We have established what shyness costs you and how it benefits you. To manage the costs and capitalize on the benefits, we need to know how to cope with anxiety that is triggered when you are put in a new social situation thanks to your shyness. But, let us find out why you are shy in the first place. Know the answers to the "whys" could help you better answer the how questions. And it is the answers you get that can put you in the best position to manage your shyness.

Socially triggered anxiety is anxiety that occurs when a shy person is put in new setting where they have to socially interact with other people. We already know the symptoms of anxiety but what are those type of social settings that can cause a person to dread being in them in the first place? Let us start from the simple stuff and build it up from there

1. Eating in public:

You would be amazed at how terrifying the prospect of sitting down in public to eat can be for some people. You ask yourself questions like, am I holding the right utensils? Are there people watching me? Are people judging me as they watch me eat?

2. Public Speaking

If you were to rank the anxiety levels activities like these would cause out of 100%, public speaking would probably be at 110% for most people. Even people who do not have problems with anxiety dread public speaking. For shy people, the feeling of dread is even worse.

3. Leading a group of people

There are people who are recognized as natural born leaders. Those kinds of people are rarely ever shy. They integrate themselves fully into the team, make it a point to recognize the strengths and weaknesses of each team member and then delegate tasks based on this knowledge. Succeeding at leadership would require interaction with people and that right there is a trigger.

4. Asking a girl out

Beautiful girls are gorgeous to look at but terrifying to talk to. And this is not about the girl in question. It is about you. Your fear of rejection makes you anticipate negative responses. You are mostly worried that she is going to say no, and that no could confirm your worst fears about what other people think of you.

5. Standing up for yourself

Shy people are not the confrontational type. Their go-to motto is "let it slide". Even in situations where their emotional well-being is threatened, the thought of standing up against those frustrating them triggers a myriad of anxiety symptoms that can go from mild to extreme.

These are just a few of these scenarios that could make you super nervous like office parties, family reunions or even just getting on a flight. But, why is it that some people are extremely shy and some people are overtly confident? Is it just the luck of the draw or are there biological influences? There are many things that contribute to making a person shy but, we are going to put them in 4 categories.

1. BEHAVIORAL CONDITIONING

They say it takes 21days to form a habit. It only takes the brain a moment to register an event and set up a series of chain reaction that conditions you to act a certain way every time said event occurs. Say for instance, you were on stage as a child and on your way to the stage, you tripped and fell. You brain registers this incident as embarrassing and every time you want to take the stage, you would re-live this embarrassing moment. Over time, you are conditioned to fear the stage and you develop anxiety attacks as soon as you think of getting on stage.

2. INDIVIDUAL THOUGHT PROCESS

My father told me once that a man is the sum total of his thoughts. If you dwell on positive thoughts, you tend to be more positive in your approach to life. You anticipate positive responses, so you are more confident in your reaction to these situations you think about. Negative reasoning elicits negative reactions and negative behavioral patterns. If you are meeting someone for the first time and you focus too much on all the terrible things they might say about you, chances are, you may not follow through on that meeting.

3. SOCIAL CONDITIONING

This has more to do with your upbringing than it has to do with you. The parenting method used by your parent or guardian shapes your social behavior. Children of aggressive and controlling parents who have a habit of criticizing every single thing the child does tend to be painfully shy in their interactions with people. That is because they have been raised to think that they are not good enough and they assume that everyone they meet is also criticizing them. It can take years of therapy and deliberate efforts to rebuild one's confidence after taking years negative criticism from a parent.

4. BIOLOGICAL REASONS

Believe it or not, some people are genetically programmed to be shy. And certain forms of anxiety can be hereditary. It may not be directly inherited from your parents. All you need is just one person in the family to have it and the markers extend to the next generation. It is not fair, but it also does not mean that your life is bound to be one terrible experience after the other. Sure, you may have some challenges and bumps along the way. But if you work at it you could go on to have a very fulfilling life.

Regardless of the reasons you are shy, the good news is that you can reverse the negative effects of shyness. It may not happen overnight, and you may have to push yourself more than a little out of your comfort zone. But, in the end, every little victory you score would make it worth it. However, there are certain self-sabotaging things you might find yourself doing that will impede your ability to make progress. I am going to list out three of them. If you find yourself doing any of these, stop.

Being too self-conscious

When you are constantly self-conscious, you feed on the illusion that people are watching you closely and criticizing you. This makes it difficult to interact with people much less be yourself around them. The reality of the situation is that while it is impossible for everyone to like you, it is just as impossible for everyone to dislike you. Even Satan who happens to be the most evil being in existence has some fans (terrible comparison but I had to go with the worst case scenario here). My point is, spending your time fretting over what people think about you is a wasted effort. Not only do their opinions not count (that is assuming they are talking about you), this kind of thinking is counter productive in building your confidence. Instead, focus on the one person's opinion who matters...yours.

Avoiding new situations

If you have been playing things safe, now is the perfect time to throw caution to the win and take a chance on you. I am not saying that you run off to the nearest cliff and begin a career as a cliff diver (although that would be immensely cool). But, you can't keep putting off things simply because you are afraid. The idea is to gain confidence by overcoming your fears. And, you cannot overcome your fears if you are doing the same things every day. It doesn't have to be something grand. Switching up your sandwich fillings every now and then counts. But, if the activity doesn't really challenge you, you are not doing yourself and favors.

Having negative thoughts

We already talked about negative thoughts and how it causes anxiety. If you want to see more positive results in your life, you are going to have to start thinking positive. Sometimes, people confuse being positive with living in denial. But, there is a huge distinction. Living in denial means seeing the truth but refusing to acknowledge it anyway. Being positive on the other hand is seeing the truth for what it is but making a choice to focus more on the positive attributes. Being a positive person is about making a conscious decision to be happy.

Overcoming Shyness in the Workplace

Your workspace is where you spend a better part of your week. Your interaction with your colleagues could help make your work experience a good one or a terrible one. We have heard horrifying stories of crazy colleagues and nightmare bosses. Some organizations have a toxic work culture that makes it difficult to navigate the workspace, even for the most confident person. That said, you can make a decision to improve your day to day experience at work while building sustainable relationships with your colleagues.

This doesn't mean you have to become BFFs with them. The objective here is to develop cordial relationships that you can capitalize on. This way, you can make more meaningful contributions to the growth of the organization and in so doing, guarantee some personal growths as well. Here are 5 things you can do to get started

1. Make eye contact

Casting your eyes downwards to avoid eye contact might be considered a sign of respect in the animal kingdom but when dealing with humans in a work environment, it is considered a sign of weakness and marks you as ripe for the picking. Studies have proven that people who make eye contact are considered confident, competent and powerful. You want your colleagues to see as these? Then you need to let your eyes do the talking even if you aren't saying much verbally. However, you should learn to work you eye contact making skills because if you keep eye contact for too long, it can quickly go from confident to creepy.

2. Say hello

Walking past your colleague without even as much as a glance or a nod is considered rude and does nothing to help your relationships at work. If not for anything else, just do it to be polite. You would be amazed at how a simple smile and a hello can change relationship dynamics at work. You don't need to launch into a long drawn out conversations. It is about connecting with people. Smiling, waving and saying hello makes you appear friendlier and more outgoing even if you really aren't. And this gives your colleagues a more positive opinion of you.

3. Introduce yourself

There was a time in my life when I would rather jump out of an airplane than walk up to a complete stranger (that I have been working with for months) and introduce myself. It wasn't until an office incident where a delivery package came for me and no one knew who I was. Not even my cubicle mates. I had become so successful at being invisible that I had worked in the firm for over a year and no one knew my full name. In retrospect, it is funny but at the time, it felt sad. If you run into a colleague by the coffee machine, introduce yourself. It is daunting at first, but with practice, it gets better.

4. Ask questions

There is a general misconception that people who ask questions are clueless. Granted, some questions might sound dumb right of the bat, but it is better to ask questions and know for sure than make epic mistakes based on assumptions. Asking the right questions in the workplace can help make you a more effective team player. Plus, it also gives you an opportunity to get to know your colleagues better (professionally speaking). The answers you get can give you insight into their position on a project, equip you with inside knowledge that could benefit you professionally and also enable you proffer the best solutions to problems.

5. Accept challenges

Don't be quick to say no. Your heart may be beating out of your chest and you may be sweating buckets, but challenges present an opportunity to show off your skills and ideas. The truth is, you wouldn't have been approached for the challenge in the first place if there wasn't the belief that you were up to it. Skip the negative thoughts and self-consciousness and focus instead on the task at hand. If the challenge involves working with other colleagues, meet up with your team mates, ask questions and most importantly, show up.

As you take your time working up the courage to start up these tasks I just listed, you should bear in mind that there are situations that require you to not let your shyness silence your voice. Because if you do, you are setting yourself up for failure and disappointment at work.

1. When someone steals your idea for a project

It is hard to imagine that someone would do this. Unfortunately, it happens more often than you know. You worked hard on a project only for someone else to take full credit for it. This is not okay.

2. When you are being wrongfully accused

Your reputation is an asset and you need to protect it. If you are being accused of doing something you did not do at work, you need to speak up and correct that information no matter how nervous it makes you. Because, accusations like these can leave a stain

3. When you are being harassed

Sadly, bullies did not stop their antics in high school. They take their sickening behavior to the workplace. And even if the bully is your boss, it does not give them the right to mistreat you. Speak up to the relevant authorities and put the bully in their place.

4. When you have an idea

If you have an idea that could benefit the company, share it. You can do it during meetings, via emails or even a written note. However, you do it, show the company that you are a valuable addition to the team. Plus, it is a major confident boost when your ideas are accepted.

Overcoming Anxiety in Social Settings

When you are in an informal setting, things are a lot more personal. And your dealings in these situations should reflect this. You could be meeting up with friends and families or even chatting up a complete stranger. The goal remains the same. To buildup on existing relationships or to create new ones. It is not always easy but, I will always say this. It is worth it.

1. Stay in the present

When we are in new social environments, our minds have a tendency to drift off to the last painful (not to mention embarrassing) incident. We relive that painful memory and then we start panicking based on this previous experience. This happens even when there are no indications that the past could repeat itself in the present. You need to stop, calm yourself down and keep yourself rooted in the "now". Resist the urge to run and teach yourself to relax.

2. Remove any illusions you have about perfections

There are no perfect situations. You can glimpse perfect moments in between but, there are no perfectly ideal situations. When you have expectations about perfections, you are setting yourself up for disappointment. Instead, keep an open mind. Sure, you want that Thanksgiving dinner to look like something out of movie but in reality, you are getting more of a Bridget Jones vibe at the table. With nosy uncles, squabbling siblings and children tantrums. Go with the flow and keep your humor hat on. This kind of thinking would make things less awkward.

3. Lay off the booze

I can understand the sense in borrowing some liquid courage to keep up your end of the conversation but, if you tip that bottle a little farther than you intended, you could end up becoming the conversation stopper. Alcohol helps you loosen your inhibitions but, that is not the only thing that can be let loose. If you are feeling nervous, admit to it. This allows you to be vulnerable and when you talk from a vulnerable place, there is a high chance that the conversations you have will be genuine. And genuine conversations are key to building meaningful relationships.

4. Try new things

The more accustomed you get to being in new situations, the quicker you adapt when these new situations arise. And with each new social skill you gain, your confidence grows. Do things that interests you. That way, you are even better motivated to take on the challenge. There are also mental benefits to trying out new things. For starters, you open up neurological pathways in your brain. This keeps you mentally fit and reduces your chances of becoming depressed. This positive frame of mind is healthy for your social behavior as people prefer to be around people who are positive minded. The bonus is, you would have tons of stories to share.

Closing

This book may have come to an end, but your journey is just beginning. There are some choices ahead for you to make.

Life is beautiful. Life is also hard. But the interesting thing is you can choose what you would rather dwell on. The beautiful side of life or the hard side of life? Being shy can be limiting in many ways but it can also be a blessing. Today, you have been given the choice to either allow your shyness to interfere with your life's experiences or enrich your life despite your shyness. I want you to be happy and live a fulfilling life. But, no matter how much I want this, you can only have that life if you want it too.

So, here is my final piece of advice to you today. Want more. Don't settle for the shadows when you can play in the light. Don't settle for the crumbs on the floor when you can enjoy the feast at your table. You are made for more and you deserve it.

How to Talk to Anyone

51 Easy Conversation Topics You Can Use to Talk to Anyone Effortlessly

Introduction

How often do you go out and meet people? Do you have problems speaking with strangers, especially during office parties and events you can't avoid attending? Do you get awkward in groups? Cat always got your tongue? You might be as introvert as the next person but talking with people is something you cannot possibly run from every single time. Humans, as social beings, are biologically wired to communicate. Language and communication play a key role in our survival and development.

Not to dwell so much on the biological and social importance of communication though, it is a truth well-known that conversing with people, especially strangers doesn't come as easily for all of us. This doesn't mean, however, that being a great and much-remembered conversationalist is an elusive dream. On the contrary, the talent for speaking is a work in progress that is not so different from learning to play the piano or starting a new hobby like dancing or stitching. It's a skill that requires practice, and surely some trial and error inserted here and there.

This book will be your headstart – a path to becoming the charismatic, interesting, and smart conversationalist who can talk with confidence with anyone, at any setting or event. It provides practical tips, and some exercises to build and strengthen your conversation muscles. Aside from the do's and don'ts you can use as a guideline of a sort in conversing, this book also shows a total of 51 topics for

James W. Williams

conversation that will definitely hook the people you talk with and make you the unforgettable guy or gal before you leave the party.

Applying the principles of this book in real life may be every bit of a challenge because the hardest part of the journey is breaking the ice hindering you from standing smoothly on the starting line. Even as you successfully make the first step and take the journey, challenges and failures will continue rocking your boat. However, not moving forward will make you a stagnant witness that remains in one place while the rest of the world changes and evolves. That is a worse scenario even if you try to look at it at every different angle. Don't be left behind! Swallow down that nervousness and flex your conversation muscles. This book will not fail you on the basics, but rather push you a little towards the center stage. Don't be afraid to get some of the spotlight for yourself.

Talk. Get to know people. BE KNOWN.

Chapter One: Communication and Development

Communication is a crucial part of a person's social development. The ability to construct words into meaningful communication is a natural skill that distinguishes us from other mammals, establishing our superior intelligence as overall species. Language and communication shape the intelligence and social skills of the speaker and the people he/she interacts with. Culture and social norms in a specific community are also defined by language. For instance, instilling a set of rules and behavioral standards at a very young age influences a person's development as a unique individual with certain traits, behavior, decision-making strategies, skills, and beliefs. It is no surprise to find these components similar to those of succeeding generations, as they are passed from parents to children.

Language and communication are also key players in emotional development. Through conversation and regular interaction with other people, a person learns not only the right words to express ideas and feelings, but also nonverbal indicators such as gestures, tone, and facial expressions that give more meaning to what is being said. Emotions are mostly expressed nonverbally through facial expressions, eye contact, and body language, but they are more understood by other people when putting words to them. Experiences made during conversations help develop empathy and social skills that are not necessarily taught and learned in books, such as analyzing subtexts and hidden meanings and appropriately responding to them in words and ways that are within the confines of what is proper and socially acceptable. Ultimately, development of cognitive, emotional, and social skills nurtures a person's growth and ability to build and sustain relationships.

Three Pillars of Communication

There are three (3) main pillars of communication every person needs to take to heart. These are non-verbal communication, conversation skills, and assertiveness.

Non-verbal Communication

Ever heard the saying, "Words are wind?" We may say things that we don't really mean. Words can be easily used to lie, control, and manipulate. They are powerful weapons, and they can be dangerous. Non-verbal signs, instinctual gestures, and body language, on the other hand, are just as powerful, or maybe even more. Words can be diverted from their true meaning, but non-verbal gestures are difficult to fake. Oftentimes, they speak more honestly than what the mouth says and therefore are more effective in putting messages across to people. To be a better conversationalist, you should watch out for hand gestures, eye contact, and facial expressions, and learn to divulge their meanings.

Communication Skills

The strongest indicator of a good conversationalist is his/her skills in communicating, not only based on how good or right he/she utilizes words to get the most desired responses from the people being talked to, but also by how he/she maintains the conversation smooth and going.

Assertiveness

Being assertive doesn't necessarily mean taking all the spotlight and being selfish in directing conversations to wherever you want without considering the feelings of other people. On the contrary, assertiveness means being honest with your own feelings, needs, ideas and wants, yet being mindful of other people's needs and opinions at the same time. Assertiveness is not settling for passive conversation, wherein you hold yourself back. Conversation is give and take, where everyone learns and grows together.

Conversing easily and being loved for it is a skill that takes a lot of practice, and even embarrassing life anecdotes. It's part of the learning curve. It's true that there are people who were born with charisma and silver tongue, but this doesn't mean that people who aren't genetically gifted with words can't be a good or exceptional conversationalist. Anyone can, but like all paths leading to grander things, there are obstacles on the way.

Fear

One of the obstacles that limit a person from being a confident speaker is fear. Some of the thoughts that fuel such fear are being judged wrongly by other people, embarrassing the self, causing misunderstanding, and unintentionally hurting others. Fear and the thoughts or events that trigger it are wired to past experiences. It is very difficult to overcome something that has been imprinted in our system. As the saying goes, "old habits die hard." Letting go of the fear that hinders you from speaking easily to others may be a huge iceberg that's impossible to even crack, but at least you can try to mellow it down to a comfortable level. How?

Rate Your Fear

Fear isn't too abstract to be assessed, especially on a personal level. Without too much thinking and drama on the backdrop, nobody knows you more than yourself. You can rate your fear based on how strong you feel it, and this is the first step to trying to control it if overcoming it seems impossible, or at least impossible at the moment. Let's try this with the following questions:

What makes you so afraid or nervous about talking to people?

When did you start having such fear? What happened back then that possibly developed your fear of talking to people?

What are the other elements you remember from that time, e.g. people, sounds, surroundings, etc?

When was the last time you felt the same fear or been in a situation very similar to the first one when your fear was triggered? What did you do? Who were you with? How did it end?

Ask these questions to yourself and feel your fear. On a scale of 0 – 10, how afraid are you? On a scale of 0 – 10, how do you think you will fare if you are in the same situation again? By evaluating the level of your fear, you establish a baseline from which you can start working from. It's difficult to assess how much effort you would invest in if you don't

Emotional Intelligence

have a point of reference. The target is to try to get further from this baseline bit by bit.

Dwell on It

When you repeatedly find yourself in the same situation, the drill becomes cumbersome and boring. It's the same with fear. If you are faced with the same fear over and over again, chances are your original fear diminishes, because somehow, you are ready and prepared to tackle it. This is especially true if you've somehow gained the knowledge on how to combat it. The repeated process is part of a learning curve, remember?

However, this step is a long stretch, so put the test on an imaginary scenario. Imagine yourself in the same situation that raises your fear. In this setting, you have the choices to act differently. How would you respond to it this time? What do you think will be the better course of action? Do you feel empowered this time? If you do, that's the first indicator that you're ready to take on the challenge of facing your fear in real life circumstances. You already have an idea on how to better act, and perhaps get a more desirable outcome. Always remember that fear is driven by your thoughts, and if you redirect your thoughts towards a path that you prefer, then you can put your fear to a place where you want it – inside a box where you can contain and control it.

Face It

You know more about your fear now and have some ideas on how to redirect it or limit its grip on your nerves. You're now much more equipped on handling it. The final stage to test your mettle in the real world. Go to a public event. Grab the opportunity to be in a setting where speaking with strangers is inevitable. Approach a few and begin with your first test.

Chapter Two: Do's and Don'ts: Basic Guide to Good and Proper Conversations

The path to becoming an exceptional conversationalist is an art in the making. Like all works of art, there are basics to follow, guidelines to adhere to, before creating your very own masterpiece. Yes, conversations are supposed to be flexible. They take different shapes and traverse various routes, depending on the people controlling them. However, basic etiquette to proper conversing exists, and it would do you good to keep them in mind and practice all the time. The basic guide of good and proper conversation is defined by the following setup.

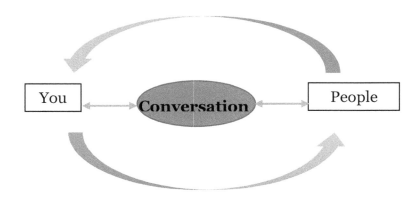

You

This set of rules is specifically for you – your actions, attitude, and behavior.

Don't steal all the spotlight.

People normally want to be the center of attention - the most interesting, the funniest, the most charismatic, the best guy/gal in the room. This is a trap – a bog of pride that will eventually push you under. While it's totally okay (sort of) to sometimes grab the spotlight when you're talking with family and close friends, the same won't cut it when you're rowing the boat on strange waters. Humans can be conceited peacocks. We want to leave a good impression wherever we go, especially in a company of strangers who have the potential to become new acquaintances or good friends, depending on how they strike that spark with you. Being a bragger or a know-it-all, typically anyone with humongous head and ego will definitely gain you enemies rather than friends.

It's not all about You.

If you think that a rip in your jeans or a wine stain on your white blouse will gain the attention and sniggers of all the people in the room, think again. Remember that in unfamiliar waters, the first and foremost in people's mind and concern is their own selves. They're probably more worried about how they will make the best impression at a party of people. With that running along the larger chunk of their brain, don't ever think that they have time to look at your shirt and pick on you for it. If you, however, find yourself being noticed for that rip or stain or whatever wardrobe malfunction, then perhaps you have your clumsiness and misfortune as starting topic for conversation and possible source of friendly laughter with strangers. This feat is quite tricky though, and you must have that cool sense of humor under your sleeves to perfectly ace it.

Empathy is Everything.

Putting yourself in someone else's shoes always gain appreciation, especially from strangers who don't have a gauge to measure you with, except the impressions they have of you on the first meeting. For instance, if the topic is a sensitive one, and you find yourself in the side of the fence opposite to that of the person you're talking to, be the proverbial cucumber and keep your horses down. You don't have to be passive, you just have to take the time to listen and see different points of view in the eyes of their believer. Even when you disagree, be courteous and kind about it. Don't lose your hair if you find yourself butting heads with an impenetrable wall of opinion. You'll have that luck of meeting some people who think and act like the world revolves around them. Be the bigger person. Part from them with unerring politeness, and a warm smile.

Be a Conduit rather than an Endpoint.

People who stay in the middle and make effort to understand their surroundings and the people in it are much more remembered in a positive way. There is this trick that most likable people have mastered to make them unforgettable. It's the ability to go with the waves of conversation and give way for other people to shine. I know someone who never fails to charm his way in the crowd. His secret? He lets the other person talk more about himself, and he makes more opportunities for that person to talk by directing the conversation toward a shared area of interest.

He never acts like a doormat, no. The man is just so open-minded that other people's interest spikes his own, and he asks questions to learn more and keep the conversation flowing.

Raise your Energy.

The magic word: ENTHUSIASM. When you feel and act enthused, it is easy to infect people with positive energy; much more if you set the energy bar higher. Remember that people want to talk about themselves. Being interested and acting like it when they do so will endear you to them. Again, there should be a balance. You don't have to forget your own opinions and desire to be known. You should also give details about yourself when the opportunity presents itself, but stay within a zone of shared interest or similar topic so as not to steal someone else's thunder.

Be an Empty Vessel.

The world has more questions than answers. When unsure of what topics to tackle to keep the conversation flowing, ask questions. Think of yourself as an empty cup waiting to be filled to the brim with new information. Asking questions can also up your endearment points because it shows your interest and enthusiasm about the people you're talking to, and your sincere want to really know them.

Conversation

Conversation, or how they're supposed to unravel, is not easy to control, and frankly, it shouldn't be. That's the fun in it – the element of surprise and sense of adventure are gifts you can unwrap with your conversation partner. Still, there are rules that proper conversation has to live by, and conversationists need to adhere to. Conversations need to be harmonious, balanced, and positive for all parties involved. They also have to stay within the confines of social standards to avoid offending or insulting anyone.

Keep it Flexible.

Conversation is like a meandering river. It can change abruptly, in direction, pace, or both. It can stop at one point. Interruptions happen, but they shouldn't discourage you from continuing where you left off, or start an altogether new topic. The trick is to be an instrument of flow, and not an obstacle. Remember the second rule for you: it's not all about you.

Don't Drop the Small Talk.

A lot of people underestimate the power of small talk. They think it too shallow or petty, and absolutely dispensable. They want to jump over the first steps and deal with the real thing immediately. Small talk is an effective starting point – an opportunity to build the conversation into something more and deeper. It provides the stage for first impressions, and for people to be acquainted. It is a chance to be well-liked from the very start.

Watch Out for Sensitive Topics.

Sensitive issues like religion, politics, and death are absolutely no-go when conversing with people for the first time. These topics have so much personal bias, and unless you're in a company of friends or people you're close to, they're not safe grounds.

People

There are a lot of helpful things you can find if you manage to observe carefully the people you're talking to. The subtle movements and expressions can tell you if the conversation is successfully and smoothly progressing. What your conversation partner does helps you determine the best ways to respond.

Check the Non-Verbal Signs.

Does your conversation partner maintain eye contact when speaking with you? Is his/her stance away from you? Are his/her arms crossed in the chest? Does he/she yawn frequently? Does he/she often look away from you when you're speaking? These are indicators of the success or failure of your conversation with someone. If the stance, eye contact, and movement or small fidgets of the person you're talking to are always away from you, that person is not interested in how your conversation is progressing and wants to get away from you as soon as the opportunity permits it. If there is yawning, it's highly likely that you bore the person. Seeing these signs, you're now faced with two choices: redirect the whole conversation towards something more interesting for the person, or drop the whole thing and gracefully part ways. You'll know how to properly react by evaluating non-verbal cues and reading words' subtexts.

Chapter Three: The Best 51: Topics to Make Easy and Interesting Conversations

A good conversation proceeds as follows:

Opener/Starter ➜ Details and Filler ➜ Ender/Exit

The opener/starter is the introduction phase. The details and the filler comprise the body of the whole conversation. It doesn't mean that the discussion at this stage of conversation traverses a single topic. Like spokes in a wheel, the procession of the conversation can go to different directions. The ender is the final say. It's not a wrap-up per se, but this is where the amicable parting of ways happens, and final impression sets in.

Opener/Starter

The most challenging part of a conversation is the opener. Oftentimes, we find ourselves struggling to strike a conversation because we don't know where to start. The opener can make or break the whole conversation process, because this might be the only chance you have to grab your prospect's attention and make a good impression. The opener is the building point of the whole conversation. Before asking any question, however, do the courtesy of **introducing yourself first**.

Killer Starters/Openers

Killer starters should be far more interesting than cliché

questions such as "Where are you from" or "What do you think will be the weather tomorrow?" For an easier topic, be straightforward in asking the person about any interesting event that highlights his/her day or week, or talking about the event or place where both of you are currently at. Using your environment and surroundings to choose possible opener topics is easier and less likely to fail, compared to asking personal questions right off the bat. The following are good examples:

1. Hi, I'm _____. How do you do?

2. Do you know the host/event organizer?

3. This event is so _____. Have you ever been to a similar event before?

4. What brings you to this event by the way?

5. This place is _____. I have been to _____ with a _____ similar to this. Where did you come from/Where do you live by the way?

6. Well, the hor d'ouvres is _____! Did you like/hate it, too? What did you like/hate best/least?

7. What do you do/What's your job?

Details/Fillers

This stage of the conversation is where you can go deeper, and a little personal, depending on the person and the situation. Based on the openers you used, you can build a chain of topics or questions that will help you know your conversation partner more, and build rapport.

For instance, if your opener topic talks about the event or the place, you can use the following questions as a guide:

This place is _____. I have been to _____ with a _____ similar to this. Where did you come from/Where do you live anyway?

8. Oh, that's too _____ from here. I'm from _____. That's where my parents live. But I stay at _____ here in the city/State. Where do you stay?

9. You have a family there?

10. Did you go to (hometown) _____'s college/university?

11. What course did you take?

12. Where do you work now?

13. What kind of work do you do/What's your job position in that company?

Do you know the host/event organizer?

14. Oh, you do? How did you meet?

15. Oh, you don't. Well, I know him/her. He/She is _____. We _____. I think if you need a good host/organizer, you can put him/her on your list. Do you know anyone from here who's as good as him/her?

16. Do you think that events business is booming nowadays? I always see posts and photos on Facebook/Instagram/Pinterest and I think they're gorgeous.

17. Do you know anyone who's into the same business?

18. Who would you recommend? Do you have their site or page/portfolio?

19. There's this _____ thing I heard/saw/experienced with an event's organizer. It was about _____. So _____ happened, and _____. Have you had the same experience? What happened?

This event is so _____. Have you ever been to a similar event before?

20. What was the most unforgettable moment you had in that event?

21. Well, you know, this kind of event is _____. I heard that _____. Can you believe that? What can you say about it?

22. Do you like/dislike how this event is progressing?

23. If there's one thing you would like to change in this event, what would it be? Why?

24. So, I've been in this event before, and this happened. You won't believe it. _____. Well, what do you think of that?

What brings you to this event by the way?

25. Do you know a lot of people here?

26. Well, I know the _____ of this event. He/She/They is/are my _____. Do you know him/her/them?

Well, the hor d'ouvres is _____! Did you like/hate it,

too? What did you like/hate best/least?

27. I had this worst food experience. So, I was at
_____ for the _____, then what happened
was _____. How about you? What's
your most unforgettable food experience?

28. All I can say is I'm an avid Food Guy/Girl. I waste my
TV time watching these food videos on Channel
_____. Do you watch them, too?

<**Additional:** I kind of hate Gordon Ramsay's guts
but you gotta give it to the man. He knows what he's
doing. What about you? What can you say about
him?>

29. I like to travel and try out different cuisines. I have
been to _____ and the food was great. Have you
been there before? Have you tried the _____? How
do you feel about it?

<**Additional:** Do you travel, too? What places have
you visited before? What happened while you were
there? Did you enjoy the food/tourist spots? I'm
planning to visit _____, too soon. What place do you
recommend? Where's the best place to stay/visit?>

30. I just thought the weirdest thing. You see when I
visited this joint/restaurant/diner in _____, they
served _____. I know right? It's kind of weird.
What's the weirdest food you ate?

What do you do/What's your job?

31. Oh, really? That sounds tough/interesting. So, what

do you usually do as a/an _____ in your company?

32. What's your company? What does it mainly do?

33. Well, I'm a/an at my company. Basically, my company is _____ and my job there is to _____. Does your company have the same function/job designation? Do you have partners in the same line of business?

34. How long have you been working in _____? What made you stay there? Where were you before? What made you quit?

35. In my case, I have been working in ____ for _____. I used to work in _____ as _____, but I decided to quit because_____. I quite like the _____ in my current work. How about you? What do you think is the main reason why employees stay loyal in one company?

36. If you're going to choose between pay and culture, what would it be? Why?

37. Well, you have a point there. I've just been reminded of one colleague who _____. He/She _____, then _____. How do you feel about that?

38. What's your most unforgettable work story?

As you can see, there are various interesting directions where your conversation can go, even if they begin from one starter topic. The secret is to be sincerely interested and enthused in knowing more about your conversation partner/s. That's why all follow-up questions should be directed towards your partner, even if they begin with telling something about yourself. The recommended pattern is: **I am/have _____. What about you/What do you think about it?**

Placing the ball in your conversation partner's court guarantees a longer, deeper and more meaningful response, instead of just getting a cutting Yes or No. This setup keeps the conversation flowing.

Ender/Exit

The ender is the second most difficult part of a conversation. When the discussion is so interesting and your group is having fun, you can't just cut it, or else you'll compromise your already established "likable impression." Whatever happens, you should have that graceful exit. How do you do that?

The secret is proper timing. If you need to be somewhere at a specific time, be sure that you are aware of the clock, and somehow have a plan on how to gracefully exit. It should be your turn in speaking before you end it, so you can say your goodbye politely.

You can nonchalantly look at your watch immediately after saying your piece, and say something like, *"Oh, look at how time flies! I was really having fun I didn't notice it. I need to go to _____ for _____."*

Always say thank you to your conversation partner for the enjoyable talk, and express your sincere hope of meeting them again in the future. In case that you want to get in touch with them soon for professional purposes such as business, leave a business card.

Art of Small Talk

As previously mentioned, small talk creates the groundwork for conversation build-up. It is an opportunity to establish good impressions and smooth flow of discussion. The art of small talk requires confidence and focus. With small talk, even the most mundane topics must become interesting, so the fate of the conversation lies heavily on the skills of the speaker. Any wrong move can result in awkwardness and possibly a disastrous aftermath.

Beginners can flex their conversation skills by going straight to small talk. It is actually the best arena for developing conversation skills, where you make errors, and find out your strengths and weaknesses. The following are examples of topics for small talk, which you can use to anyone, anytime, anywhere:

39. Weather

Yes, yes. Weather is a cliché topic for small talk. Its commonness is actually its charm, and the reason why it's universally expected to be the first in the list of small talk starters. It works almost all the time, so why not use it? Whether it's sunny, windy, or wintry, it's weather, and you can easily think of a dozen topics about it.

- Well I say, this constant rain of cats and dogs has been getting worse every day. I'm having problems getting my clothes dry, I don't know if I have a pair of pants to wear tomorrow. Do you think we might be seeing some ray of sunshine next week?

• Gosh, this snow is crazy! How's your car/pathway/roof? I thought I was getting out of an igloo when I walk out of my house this morning. I had to shovel ice from my pathway and car. Had any problem getting out today?

40. People

There is no limit to the number of topics you can come up for small talk when you look around. Case in point: People. There are billions of people in the world today, each with a different personality, different focus or subject of attention. So, when you see a person you want to strike a conversation with, take a look around and see what the other people are doing. Remember though: **Be Nice.**

• Would you look at that, how many dads today have much time to play with their daughters? You got kids? How many?

• See that guy over there? That's Mr. _____, an old baker across the street where I live. He makes these flaky croissants with cream fillings every single morning and sells them with free brewed coffee. It's fantastic. Have you tried them out before? Where do you buy your bread around here? Do you live near?

41. Sceneries

Similar to a variety of topics you can get by using people as subjects, your surroundings provide as many possible topics for small talks. You just have to be creative in picking one and focusing on it to come up with good follow-up topics/questions and keep the conversation smooth and flowing.

- This park is nice, right? Fresh air, lots of trees. You should see it during the fall. The leaves of those big trees near the lake turn red and burgundy in color. Are you from around here, by the way? Oh, where do you stay?/Oh, where are you from?

- See those birds over there? I heard that those migrate as far as _____ before the winter season. You know what they are called? Are you from around here?

- Brings back a lot of childhood memories? Which one do you like most, the swings or the slide? You used to have one near your home when you're a kid? Got kids of your own?

42. Events/Seasons

Anything special about the season or an event such as a holiday, New Year's, etc. is an easy topic to start a small talk with anyone.

- It's that time of the year again, I guess. First time to spend Christmas here?

- Not much to do during Thanksgiving in this part of the city. How's Thanksgiving going on with the family?

43. Personal Experiences/Details

This one is rather tricky, and has the risk of sounding invasive of someone's privacy, especially if you're talking to a stranger. If you're adept in finding out a person's character by just a glimpse and short observation, then you can easily decide if you'll go straight to personal questions or not.

- You seem to be carrying the world in your shoulders, lad. Care to share what's bothering you?

- You look like a very interesting guy/girl. Care to tell me something about yourself?

44. Common Ground

It's quite easy to strike a conversation with a stranger when you have something common at that exact moment, say, attending the same event, being introduced by a common friend or drinking at the same bar. Aside from the ease and comfort felt by both parties, the topics to choose from are various and diverse.

- Hi, are you enjoying the conference? What engineering club are you in?

- How did you know Bob? He's been my friend for 10 years, and it's my first time meeting you.

45. Current Events

Current events such as what's happening in the news lately is an easy pick for small talk starters. Try to mellow down on the opinions, however, and again, practice empathy and patience.

- All these fuel hikes, you'd believe it's better to just get back to bikes and carriages. What do you think? How's it affecting you?

- Can't believe what's happening to Indonesia right now. Earthquakes like that are sure scary. Have you seen the news? Ever experienced a scare like that?

46. Work

Talks about work is a safe enough ground where both parties can be neutral and the flow of conversation leans more on descriptive rather than opinionated. Typical follow-up questions are queries about the company, including its type of business and culture (refer to items 31 – 38).

47. Sports/Games

Imagine that you're sitting in a bar, watching a football game while drinking a beer just like anyone else. Expectedly, the place will be energized and have a fun atmosphere, so it's quite easy to make some small talks with everyone. Watching a game in a stadium might be too noisy to create long discussions with peer spectators, but small talks are easy to make. The latest NBA playoff game with your favorite team playing, or the Olympics that has just started are good samples of small talk starters when your prospect conversation partner is a stranger, and you decided to get a conversation going in a "non-sport" place.

- Timberwolves won the last game. Yay! You into basketball? What's your team? Why do you like that team? Who's your favorite player?

48. Music

Music is a universal like, of all ages, every generation, every nation. It's quite difficult to encounter a person who hates music in general, so it's a safe enough topic for general conversation. Still, you'd need to look for things around that will fit into the music context. You can't just blurt out talks about music unless something at the moment can be linked to it. For instance, if you're in a coffee shop that plays an interesting bossa nova playlist, you can use that as a starter for music-oriented small talk.

- (Music playing in the background): This is a good song. Do you know its title? How about the artist? You don't seem/seem to be interested in this kind of genre, what genre are you into? Why do you like that? Do you have a music influence or something?

49. Hobbies and Crafts

Topics about arts, hobbies, and crafts are usually comfortable to use for small talks if you happen to be in an event or a place where similar hobbyists or artists are attending. It's a good opportunity to get interested in new things, probably try them out or learn about them while having fulfilling conversations with perfect strangers. It's also easy to endear yourself to other people and possibly gain friends or professional partners because you honestly act enthused as you try to learn more about other people's interests.

- I've always wanted to try beekeeping! I'm a sucker for pure, raw honey, but it's very difficult for me to do that. I live in the city, at a 10-storey building. How do you do it? Do you think it's possible to try that out in my place? How?

50. World Issues

World issues can be very sensitive topics. They require tact, courtesy, and empathy when being discussed with other people, especially strangers. Opinionated topics are good sources of long, fulfilling and smart conversations, but they can be tricky if (1) you're not familiar with the topic; (2) there is social diversity (ethnicity/race, religion, political leaning, etc.) involved; and (3) you have experiential lack/disadvantage. In such cases, the best way is to act as an empty vessel and a conduit, aside from the expected practice of tact and consideration, at all times.

By being in the middle ground, you're able to see different sides of the story, multiple facets of an idea, and opposite perspectives of people. Not only do you gain knowledge about the topic, but friends as well. Furthermore, if unsure, always ask questions. It's better to admit ignorance but with a willingness to learn, rather than pretend that you know things.

51. Anything Under the Sun

Everything around us has its own different stories. Stories are always exciting treasures to discover, new places to explore, new experiments to tinker with. The quiet man you always pass by when you go to your favorite bakery, the little dog that barks at you at the park, the ancient tree standing at your neighbor's front yard – these are stories that are already made, yet you can make them or alter them or create something more out of them. The choice, the ways – they're endless.

Chapter Four: Flex Your Conversation Muscles

As cliché as it sounds, practice do make perfect, and conversation skills direly need a regular muscle-flexing to grow and develop. In the previous chapters, you have been taught about fear, including how to assess yours and bring it to manageable levels. You also have tips on how to start with small talks and progress in conversations, from starter to ender, right under your sleeve. Now it's time to apply what you've learned to the real world.

Breathe deeply. Relax. Begin the Introductions. Now here are some of the additional tips to remember while you're having conversations:

First-Name Basis

Saying the other person's name, or in case of conversing with a group, the other people's names, puts them at ease and endears you to them. It shows that you make time to remember their names and are sincere in really knowing them.

Just Yes or No is a No-no

A single "yes" or "no" for an answer is a roadblock both parties will have trouble in overcoming. It's awkward, especially if no follow-up question arises. Be creative in the next questions you will ask. Make them talk longer. When they ask you a question, end your answer with a question, too.

Be Natural

Humans are naturally smart in getting the subtexts, reading non-verbal cues, and finding out more thru instincts. Be honest and sincere from the very beginning, and you can easily break someone's wall.

Conclusion: Going Beyond with the Power of Conversation

Assertiveness is one of the major pillars of communication. As mentioned, it is putting across, in a nice and proper way, your needs and desires in the conversation. It's your way of not being left out in the conversation. Hence, in a way, you should exert control and dominance on the conversation, and where it goes. This is called influence, which is driven by the following factors: emotion, expertise, positional power, and control over the interaction *(Source: Nick Morgan, Conversation and Extend Your Influence, https://www.forbes.com/sites/nickmorgan/2013/04/25/how-you-can-dominate-the-conversation-and-extend-your-influence/#264bf36b7ba0)*.

Emotion

Nick Morgan emphasizes the use of passion to influence the flow of conversation. In fact, passion can sway people, as we are emotional beings. Despite power and position, there is a heart that works there somewhere, that responds to emotions and listens to empathetic pleas. Passion with patience, in particular choosing the right moment to speak and when to leave a lasting impression, is a powerful tool.

Expertise

Passion is more powerful if you put expertise on the mix.

Expertise strengthens confidence, and confidence gives a person more voice – the power to be heard. However, confidence can be dangerously used to cover up ignorance, and expertise without confidence pushes you to the back door.

Positional Power

Positional power gives a person an edge, the expected right to speak and dominate a conversation. People knows and respects authority, and that automatically offers the floor for leading a conversation.

Interaction

Even if it's the subtlest aspect of influence, it is the most difficult to master, and perhaps the strongest of the four. In fact, this aspect can be easily used to manipulate, not only the conversation but also the people involved, their responses and reactions. This aspect doesn't just make use the power of words, but the ability to read non-verbal cues, especially body languages. The secret of this aspect is the understanding of people in general – what makes them tick, what makes them disagreeable – and using this to create a conversation that is harmonious, fulfilling, and interesting, yet still largely under your control.

James W. Williams

Social Skills

Simple Techniques to Manage Your Shyness, Improve Conversations, Develop Your Charisma and Make Friends In No Time

Introduction

You could feel countless eyes staring right at you. You become immobilized. You wish the stage will open and swallow you up! How in God's name did you get yourself into this awkward situation? You open your mouth but the words won't come out. You can hear someone from the audience say "Speak up you dummy!" and your legs start to quake. You feel the bile from the pit of your belly and you rush off the stage.

Although not all of us are public speakers, I know that to some degree, you can relate with the shy and inexperienced imaginary character above that was experiencing the seemingly daunting task of his first-time on stage in front of an audience. It is not an experience to look forward to. Trust me, I know.

Interacting with people as individuals or as a group is a very difficult proposition for many people. To some, it is a very debilitating experience that they would rather avoid by all means. But for communication between humans to be effective, good social skills must be employed. After all, we as humans are social creatures with an inborn need to interact with other humans.

A lot of people suffer from shyness and lack of charisma and this directly impacts negatively on their ability to interact socially. This can result in low self-esteem and a poor self-image. You may know of a person who became socially withdrawn or is a lone wolf because of their lack of good social skills. They feel out of place when they find themselves in the midst of people or they find it extremely awkward when there is a need for them to say a simple "hello" especially to a stranger.

We may not all be introverts or excessively shy. And we may not all want to be public speakers or the center of attention in the midst of social gatherings. But we all do need good social skills in order to enjoy the company of our friends, family and even strangers. The good news is: being shy is not a death sentence. You can actually develop your social skills little by little or at a pace that is comfortable for you.

Perhaps you have read books about social skills that all sounded bogus and filled with vague tips; or maybe you are almost giving up and recoiling into your shell of timidity; or you are in search for a book that shows you the exact tips and the "how to" of becoming great with your social skills; whatever your case, this book is guaranteed to give you the boost of confidence you need to relate with people, make new and amazing friends, communicate effectively, and most importantly, give you a sense of belonging in your world.

Let me be realistic here and tell you upfront: you are not going to become great with your social skills overnight or by simply reading a book. Work is required on your part. You need to be committed to improving your skills and stick to it until you achieve your desired results.

From my experience and the experiences of millions of other people, it is certain that things happen for us in accordance with who we are; happy things search for happy people and happen to them. Amazing things look for amazing people and happen to them. Lonely, withdrawn, and unsure people... well, let's just say they aren't as happy as they know they could be. For exciting things to happen for you, you need to go out and mix up with exciting people; let their energy of excitement rub off on you. Then, exciting things can happen to you.

Lots of people have used the exact same tips and techniques I share in this book to transform their almost nonexistent social life into an amazing lifestyle donned with the right kinds of people they so desire.

It is time to put an end to that awkward feeling of social anxiety or social phobia. Take a leap into a new world of endless possibilities as you read and apply my "how to" techniques on improving your social skills.

Chapter 1: Overcoming Shyness

Obviously, the first step in improving your social skills is overcoming shyness. I mean, you don't teach a shy person how to charm others or how to make friends quickly without first showing them how to beat their shyness.

I will not bore you with some synopsis of what shyness is or the negative effect of shyness. You probably know the effect which is why you are reading this book. Everyone knows that shyness can wreck a person's chances at work, in relationships, at school, in social gatherings, and generally in relating with other people. And no one likes that uncomfortable and timid feeling shyness brings. So let's delve straight into how to overcome shyness with the proven techniques below.

How to Beat One-On-One Shyness

Having one-on-ones can trigger a lot of uncomfortable feelings for a shy person. One-on-ones can be with your boss (very disquieting), a stranger (very creepy), your in-laws (very awkward), or someone you have a crush on (very unnerving). This can quickly reflect visibly in your body: heartbeats increases, palms get sweaty, temperature increases, face flushes, you begin to fidget uncontrollably – it's almost a pitiable sight to behold!

Basically, to overcome this you need to take charge of the reactions in your body. Those reactions are your senses screaming at you to take cover because they sense you are stepping into a "danger zone." It is their way of protecting and keeping you safe. Take charge by telling your senses that you've got this under control. Here's how you do that.

1. Take deep breaths: when faced with one-on-one, take controlled and deep breaths, holding the breaths in a bit longer than you would normally do before letting it out slowly. When you do this, you tell your nerves to calm down. It is a way of asserting your authority; making your body realize that you are in charge and they (your nervous system and its sensors) can rest easy. Breathing deeply has a way of relieving you of built up stress and anxiety. It also allows you to think more clearly.

2. Adjust your body posture: you can sniff out a shy person from a mile away by the way they carry themselves. When faced with one-on-one, don't let your head down – literally, don't! Keep your head upright and look straight ahead or at the person. Broaden your shoulders and keep your elbows and arms away from your ribs. And whatever you do, do not let your hands go into your pockets! That's a dead giveaway that you are nervous. And once your body receives this nervous signal, you can be sure it will shut down other body systems to protect you from this perceived "danger." Get a good grip of the message your body language is passing. Adjust your posture to show confidence rather than submissiveness. Notice any tensed muscles in your body and loosen them up by tightening and relaxing them repeatedly for a few seconds. And by all means no hunching! Stand up

tall or sit up (except when you choose to lean back to show confidence).

3. Shift your focus away from you: here's the thing; we all have inadequacies and flaws, but to a person having a large dose of insecurity or lack of self-confidence their attention is usually riveted on their own shortcomings. Their feeble mind continuously chatters and deafens them with loud screeches of "you are not good enough," "you can't do that," so they automatically place their focus on their perceived defects whenever they are in contact with a person whom they assume is better than them in some way. To overcome these so-called flaws of yours, shift your attention to something other than you when you are having a one-on-one. Give your attention to your surroundings, the in and out of your controlled breaths, or any other thing aside from your weaknesses. Well, actually not any other thing really because that may distract you from conversations that may occur during your one-on-one. Basically, I will recommend that you shift your attention away from you to the other person. What are they saying? How are they carrying themselves? What can you emulate from them? Is there something you like about them? When conversing during one-on-ones, give your mind some task by allowing yourself to be curious. Let your curiosity show up in the questions you ask. This way, your mind will not be focused on you but on the other person.

How to Get Over Shyness at Work or at School

The workplace and school are two places most people (adults and young people) spend a lot of their waking hours. This means that shy persons are always in a closed community where their reputation for shyness can spread really fast. This is an added pressure to the shy person.

Okay, so how do you survive under such pressure as a shy person? How do you not cringe and drift back more into your shell? Here's how:

1. Become an expert: have you noticed how the go-to guy in the office seems to have an extra dose of self-confidence? Well, his confidence level wasn't always that way until people began tumbling over themselves to get to him because of what he can help them do. And have you noticed how the student who is good at what he or she does seem to never lack other students flocking around them? Being good at what you do whether at work or in school is a great way to help you overcome shyness because it opens you up to social interactions with the people that seek your expertise. It may appear that you are at the giving end of these interactions as you are offering something they need. But in the actual sense, it's a win-win relationship because you are equally building your self-confidence and learning better ways to interact with people and socially integrate with your peers. It's kind of what students would refer to as a symbiotic relationship and working-class persons would call a mutually beneficial liaison. So get to work on that skill, talent, hobby, subject, course, or whatever it is you have a

flair for and become really good at it. People at work or school are sure to notice and come flocking around you.

2. Deliberately put yourself forward: did I mention you have to be determined in your efforts to overcome shyness? Well, you do have to be determined. Shyness cannot be wished away; neither can you think it away. One way to show your determination is to choose to put yourself forward by participating in things that would normally scare the living daylight out of you. Offer to give a presentation in class or at work; walk up to a group of colleagues or classmates and join in the conversation; offer to host the next office or class party; just do something, anything that being shy has kept you away from doing. Challenge your shyness. Put it on the spotlight. Yes, you may fail and falter the first few times, but that's how we all learn to walk right? You didn't just get up as an infant and began strutting about. You fell and probably banged your head a couple of times. But your determination to walk kept you going until walking became natural for you. However, I recommend that you start putting yourself forward with little baby steps. You don't want to jump into things that the failure level will be so massive that it completely shuts down whatever little zest that has begun to build up in you. Take your challenge step by step. Avoid quantum leaps.

3. Timeliness: I just said take baby steps in your fight against shyness. One way to not do that is by being late for work or class. What does being late have to do with not taking baby steps? It has everything to do with it. Here's how. Picture how you will feel as a shy person walking into the class when lectures have already begun or walking into

the conference room when the meeting is well underway: all eyes on you, right? You feel like disappearing because of the unwelcome attention. Your steps begin to falter as you walk to your seat; you get clumsy and fumble with your books or folders and stuff. You have bitten more than you can chew; you have inadvertently placed yourself on the spotlight because you did not take baby steps! Lesson: be on time. Do not give your shyness trigger more reason to shut down when you are in the presence of people.

4. Participate more: the thing is you cannot overcome shyness by avoiding social activities. Thankfully, school and work offer a good number of social activities that can help you outgrow shyness if and only if you decide to participate in such activities. Beat obscurity by stepping out of the shadows and participate in social activities. I am not suggesting that you should strive to become the prom queen or the most communicative staff of the year (although that isn't entirely a bad goal for a shy person!), I am simply stating the obvious: become more open to take part in activities that expose you to learn how to be free with other people.

How to Get Your Voice to be Heard

Shy people are always quiet as if in a hush-hush attitude. Well, they are not hushing because they are keeping some vital secret that is capable of sending us all into extinction if exposed! No. They are quiet because most of their conversations take place in a realm that is not physical – in their head. And a large chunk of that conversation is negative chatter.

Being quiet or habitually speaking in a low tone is a sign of shyness. If you are not sure whether or not you speak with a low voice, here's a sure fire way to find out: ask someone if your voice is always low. Another way to know you speak in a low tone is if you are often asked to repeat yourself, or you are often misunderstood. If people usually have to lean towards you before they get what you are saying, you definitely are the hush-hush shy type.

To be socially active (at least to a healthy degree), you need to learn how to literally get your voice to be heard; you need to practice how to raise your voice. And this is how to do that:

1. Breathe deeply before opening your mouth to speak

2. Let your voice spring up from deep inside your belly or diaphragm (just don't be too obvious about this; it'll make you appear as if you want to puke).

3. Allow your words to form clearly and let them fall off your lips in a distinct manner.

4. Speak using a good pace; not too slowly and not in a hurriedly jumbled pace.

5. Make a habit of speaking to someone across the room; it will definitely make you speak louder.

General Suggestions on How to Overcome Shyness

Let me bring this chapter to a close by suggesting a few other simple tips for overcoming shyness.

1. Applaud yourself: your mind has a way of getting you to repeat something that gives you pleasure. When you commend yourself for the efforts (no matter how little) you put into overcoming shyness, your mind takes notice of the good feeling you get from that applause and shows you better ways of doing those actions that made you commend yourself. In other words, your mind helps you become better the next time you do that same thing or it opens you up to more opportunities to do that same thing in a better way. This is a great way to improve from being a shy person to a more outgoing person. So, get in the habit of taking a moment at the end of each day to applaud yourself for saying "hello" to a complete stranger, or for maintaining eye contact with another person as they conversed with you, or for responding to a question in a class.

2. Practice meditation: yes, I know that meditation is a spiritual practice but it has a way of calming our minds and quieting our train of thoughts. Since shy people usually battle with negative self-talk, meditation will help to reduce these unpleasant mental talks and refocus the mind to overcome anxiety and shyness.

3. Meet physically with real humans: it is easy to confuse social media interactions with real-life human interactions. Shy people are not dumb! In fact, they are very good with words; only not spoken words. So you can be good at expressing yourself in writing especially online but that does

not necessarily mean you are good at real-life socializing. Get in touch with real humans physically and interact. That is how to overcome shyness.

4. Learn conversation skills: conversation skills are part of social skills. Social skills build self-confidence. Self-confidence and shyness are far removed from each other. Learning conversion skills is a major way to help you overcome shyness. Go to social events, listen to conversations, and pick up tips about public speaking – that's how to learn conversation skills.

One quick word about public speaking: although this book does not aim to make everyone a public speaker, it is important to mention that many of the skills required to be a good public speaker are also the essential skills for being good at conversations. Thankfully, the next chapter is on how to improve your conversation skills.

Chapter 2: How to Improve Your Conversation Skills

Conversation is a way of bonding. It should be the most natural thing for social beings like humans who use words in communication. But alas! Some of us have a serious phobia for engaging in conversations. Your conversation skills definitely need improving if you are having a conversation with the following questions popping up in your head: what should I say next? Should I talk now or do I wait for him/her to speak?

Okay, so what do you do to make conversations flow naturally? Here are some awesome tips for improving your conversation skills.

Keep the Flow

Uneasy pauses are a sign of poor conversation. It shows that someone (or some people) is anxious about the interaction. To keep the conversation flowing:

1. Avoid eliciting one-word responses: "fine," or "it was great," are the kind of responses you get to the question, "how was your day?" and it ends there. But when you frame the same question like this, "what did you do today?" the person answering the question is free to talk for as long as they wish.

2. Leave out the superficial questions: to make conversations meaningful and worthwhile, don't flood your talk with superficial questions such, "do you think the

weather will be great tomorrow?" Dig deeper with your questions – be up close and personal if you have to (and when the other person is comfortable with it).

3. Share so that they also want to share: remember you are having a conversation and not an interview. Flooding your conversation with question after question is still a sign of poor conversation. Instead of only asking questions, interject direct questions by saying something about yourself or a situation that makes the other person want to also tell you about themselves or a situation. You do not limit the other person by requiring them to answer your question and stop. You give them the chance to ask you questions, share their opinion about what you have said, or share a similar story to yours.

Open Up

So, you want to create a good bond with a stranger or someone you barely know and hit it off with a great conversation; be ready to be open. The more you open up and let them know about you, the more they will flow with you and also open up to you. How then do you open up as a way of improving your conversation skill?

1. Talk about yourself: talking about yourself (not in a conceited manner) will give your listener the clue that you want to be friends with them or you want to connect with them. Talk about your opinions, your life, and even your feelings and in turn, your listener will likely share about themselves too. Be mindful not to give out too much information too soon though.

2. Understand yourself: you cannot properly talk about yourself – your interests, opinions, beliefs, motivations, fears, etc – if you do not know them (and you will be surprised at the number of people who don't know themselves!) For your conversation to flow and bonds with others to grow stronger, there must be knowing of each other. So do your part by understanding who you are.

Listen Actively

Conversation is not just talking nonstop. In fact, too much talking shows your conversation skills need brushing up. There is a place – a huge place for listening in a conversation. Here's how to listen actively:

1. Repeat when necessary: to show the other person you are immersed in what they have shared with you, repeat what they have told you using your words, and then you can proceed to add your opinions or suggestions and even ask more questions.

2. Nod: give nods to show that you are not just hearing their words, but also paying attention to what they are saying and are tuned into them. But don't overdo it. Nodding too much show you are not paying attention but just trying to please them.

3. Clarify with questions: to show the other person that you are actively listening and following the conversation, intermittently ask clarifying questions. You could say "What precisely are you referring to when you say…." or something along that line.

4. Listen; don't bother about your response... yet: a conversation is not an inquisition so relax and listen to what the other person is saying. Thinking about your response while the other person is still talking shows you are not fully paying attention. Practice holding off responding for a few seconds after the other person has finished talking.

Chapter 3: How to Develop Your Charisma

Being good at what you do is great, however, without charisma, you probably won't excel at what you do. Countless musicians, performers, leaders, and great speakers have had the need to improve their charisma in other to become charming to their audiences. And yes, charisma can be developed or improved upon. I know and acknowledge that some people are naturally more charismatic than others, but that does not mean a less charismatic person cannot improve on their charisma. Let's just skip the preamble and head straight to how this can be done, shall we?

Engage Attention

You can tell when someone isn't given you their full attention, right? Perhaps they perceive you as boring? Or maybe you have not done enough to hold their attention. When you truly engage people's attention, they tend to stay glued to you and everything you have to say or present from start to finish. Great preachers, leaders, and musicians have this effect on their audiences. Here's how to engage attention:

1. Facial expression and gestures: what you say has more effect if there is an equally effective facial expression behind the words. Practice different facial expression with a close friend and ask for feedback. If you are not comfortable doing

this in front of a friend, practice in front of a mirror. Use animated gestures too to give impact to your words.

2. Be present: if you truly want to engage someone's attention, put your devices on silent, keep them away or switch them off completely. The moment you begin to switch between humans and devices, you disengage from them. Also, remember to nod intermittently to show them you are present and listening.

3. Read emotions: play a video clip, preferably a clip you have not watched before, but mute the sound. I bet with a little bit of observation, you'll be able to figure what's happening in the clip. Now take that ability to observe with you as you step into social situations. By observing people's reactions you will be able to deduce unspoken cues and read their emotions.

4. Eye contact: the eyes have been said to be the window to the soul. When you look directly in the eye of whomever you are interacting with, you connect deeper with them. To create a sense of sincerity, competence, honesty, and confidence in your audience (individual or group) maintain eye contact with them for the most part of your interaction. Avoiding eye contact can seriously damage your charisma.

Affect Your Audience

Increase your charisma by influencing your audience in a powerful way. You really want to be perceived as a powerful and influential individual? Use these tips:

1. Confidence comes from knowledge: how well do you know what you know? How versatile and resourceful are you? And how many facts do you know about the things you know? You cannot come across as a confident person when your knowledge is very scanty. To boost your self-confidence, get to know a little about as many things as possible. Your self-confidence will definitely create an aura around you that influences people.

2. Pose: have you wondered why comical superheroes stand with their arms akimbo? It is a pose that conveys authority. Use poses that say "I'm in charge" to influence your audience. You can practice standing with both hands on your waist; or standing up, leaning forward and placing your hands on a table in front of you (very effective for showing authority in a meeting); or you can place your hands at the back of your head while you lean far back into your chair (don't use this pose with your boss or in-laws!).

3. Poise: have poise; compose yourself. Have a controlled grace in your movements, gestures, and body language. Keep your hands still when talking. Don't fidget. Avoid excessive nodding. And keep away from too much speech hesitations such as uh… or um… verbal fillers indicate uncertainty and doubt – something you do not want to portray if you must improve your charisma.

4. Talk little: talking too much and rapidly is not a quality of an influential person. When you speak, talk unhurriedly. Make your words scarce and make them count. That way when you speak people know the value of your words and they listen.

Making the Awkward Behavior Go Away

A lack of charisma tends to lead people to behave in a socially awkward manner. Imagine an upcoming musician with a great debut album standing on stage for the first time then fumbling with the microphone. He or she may have great talent but a poor charisma. When you feel out of place as you interact with friends, colleagues, or strangers, it makes you act oddly or clumsily. If that is the case, you need to improve your charisma to make the awkwardness go away. Here's how:

1. Socialize more: practice, they say, make perfect. Running away from places or situations that make you feel awkward will not make the awkwardness go away. You need to confront that fear by going to more social events. But do remember to go these events or gatherings with the aim of practicing how to interact with other people.

2. Stop worrying about your behavior: it's like this – the more your worry about being awkward, the more awkward you become. Relax. Be yourself. "But how can I be myself when I am awkward?" You are a work in progress so you are not awkward unless you label yourself that way. When you start believing that nothing can possibly go wrong in social situations, you give room for the best in you to blossom.

3. Fitness: what? Getting fit? Well, I know this may not be your typical charisma advice but look at this way. People who are overly worried about their physical looks tend to be

too self-conscious during social interactions to think about charming people. In fact, they don't usually feel they have any charm in them. So yes, work on being fit (physical exercises, neat outward appearance, basic social etiquettes, etc) so you won't be bothered about inadequacies during social interactions.

Closing

Social skills are inescapable if you must enjoy the richness that life has to offer. Life does not happen in isolation; an abundance of friends and warm companions, great and new opportunities, and exciting life experiences do not happen to us when we back ourselves into obscurity because we lack the necessary social skills to explore life.

I have seen people miss out from life due to shyness, poor conversation skills, anxiety, and a plain lack of charisma. These are things this book has taken into consideration and offered tested suggestions on how to improve upon.

I encourage you to put to practice the techniques you have learned in this book. Don't be afraid or feel daunted by the idea of taking up a public speaking course. Heck, you can even practice in front of your mirror! Public speaking has a direct correlation on developing your social skills. Remember that you do not have to be a professional speaker or even aim to become one, to do this.

It is a wise practice to give a presentation every once in a while to sharpen your skills. You can volunteer to speak to your local youth to pass on some wisdom you have, or you can volunteer to teach your circle of friends something you are good at. While it is okay to form clear mental images in your mind and practice conversations in your head, it is equally important to form the habit of sharing who you are with the people around you. Don't just get good at explaining inside of your head. Let those around you get to actually hear you talk about the ideas in your head.

I'll not fail to mention that you may face rejection! But hey, that's a great way to improve your self-confidence. As you bounce back from rejection and seeming failure, you will get better at handling rejection.

One beautiful thing about stepping out and practicing what you have learned in this book is that it helps you improve on emoting; you get better at expressing your ideas and yourself. Suddenly, you no longer feel uncomfortable talking with people you don't know; a world of endless and limitless possibilities is laid bare before you. The world and the people in it become a familiar playground where you have absolute freedom to express your true and inner self.

Thank you

Before you go, I just wanted to say thank you for purchasing my book.

You could have picked from dozens of other books on the same topic, but you chose this one.

So, a HUGE thanks to you for getting this book and for reading all the way to the end.

Now, I want to ask you for a small favor. **Could you please consider posting a review? Reviews are one of the easiest ways to support the work of independent authors.**

This feedback will help me continue to write the type of books that will help you get the results you want. If you enjoyed it, please let me know!

Lastly, don't forget to grab a copy of your free bonus book *"Bulletproof Confidence Checklist."* If you want to learn how to overcome shyness and social anxiety and become more confident, this book is for you.

Just go to:

https://theartofmastery.com/confidence/

Lightning Source UK Ltd.
Milton Keynes UK
UKHW010825021019
350864UK00016B/1351/P